TRACKING TRUTH

TRACKING TRUTH

AN

ALCHEMICAL

JOURNEY OF

LEARNING

FROM NATURE

DANIEL CLARK

To nature

Published by Spiritual Performance
New Mexico, USA

Ebook ISBN: 979-8-9953968-1-9
Paperback ISBN: 979-8-9953968-0-2
First Edition

This book is intended for educational and informational purposes only and is not intended as medical advice.

For more information about the author and his work, visit:
www.spiritualperformance.net

NATURE'S CALL

Nature was always calling to me. At first, it wasn't a voice, but a feeling. A magnetic pull I couldn't shake, beckoning me to follow.

That feeling pulsed through me in my youth. I couldn't understand it. I only knew that ignoring it felt like a betrayal of something vital, something ancient and true.

So if you've ever felt that quiet pull toward the natural world—if you've ever sensed there is more, waiting to be discovered—this book is for you.

Let's begin at the trailhead, where it all started.

With fire.

FIRE

1: IGNITION

My hands are engulfed in blue flames, and I'm in full-blown panic. To a bird perched in a nearby tree, the scene must look absurd: a fully grown, two-hundred-pound man with a scruffy beard screaming and flailing like an infant.

Amid the chaos, an image flickers in my mind—Prometheus: stealing fire, not to burn, but to awaken.

The morning air is sharp and pine-sweet, clinging to my skin as I stumble backward. The mountains watch silently, stone-faced and unflinching. I don't yet know what's happening or why. All I feel is searing pain, electric and consuming, jolting my mind into a frenzy.

The flames are blue because it's an alcohol fire. Its origin? My own stupidity. I had poured fuel into an already burning camp stove. The flame raced up the stream and kissed my hand, which already had some alcohol on it from my own careless handling.

The fire dies within seconds, but the pain lingers, writhing and sharp. Minutes pass before I can breathe comfortably again. I let out a few heavy sighs, trying to release the tension coiled inside my body. So much for my Rocky Mountain high.

I feel the land pulsing with judgment—cold, indifferent, even disapproving. I sit on a rock, gutted by frustration.

What am I doing out here in the Colorado wilderness? What a young, dumb, dreamy romantic I am, thinking I could hack it alone with so little experience.

I think back to my childhood room and how I'd fantasize about living in the wild, so sure of myself. Now I just feel humiliated in my ignorance. Terrible thoughts begin to surface:

I'll probably get lost and starve to death. Or worse—end up as bear food. Either way, I can already see the headline back home: Star Athlete Dies Tragically in Hiking Accident. *This will be my legacy.*

Another starry-eyed young man swallowed by the wild. In contrast to heroic tales told of summiting impossible peaks and fending off mountain lions from innocent children, mine will be cautionary. The tale of a foolish Jersey boy who overestimated himself and earned the ultimate humbling.

Even the land seems to laugh at me. I swear I can feel it mocking my naivety, urging me to flee.

But eventually, the storm inside me begins to settle. My breath slows. I start to tune back into my senses. The crisp mountain air slides down my throat, the icy texture numbing my cheeks.

Somewhere beneath the chaos, I feel a faint ember of peace. It's just enough to remember that I'm in the mountains, not the classroom. And for a moment, the fact that I'm sitting on a rock, breathing mountain air, and not stuck inside in a chair calms me.

Then the ache sets in. My lower back throbs from sitting in too deep a squat. At twenty, my body shouldn't feel this old, but fifteen years of martial arts and weightlifting have worn it raw. My toes curl in search of warmth inside my barely insulated boots.

I stare at the snow-covered ground, and in my mind's eye I see the softer forest floor I had fallen asleep on just twelve hours ago: dark soil, leaf litter, no snow in sight. The memory feels impossibly far away.

A fresh wave of exasperation builds in my chest. I try to fight it off, grasping for the *why* that brought me here. I force myself to remember the images from guidebooks, the dreamscapes that lit up my daydreams. I picture peaceful alpine vistas just beyond the next ridge.

But I can't hold the vision. The cold, the doubt, the aches in my body all collapse upon me. The discomfort overtakes my mind and gut. Irritated and anxious, I stand up to try to shake it off.

And then I realize I have no idea where the trail is. I hadn't expected snow in May, though I should have. I definitely hadn't considered it might erase the trail entirely.

Isn't the famous Colorado Trail well-traveled? Shouldn't I be able to see it carving its stream-like path through the landscape, even under snow? Aren't there supposed to be markers on the trees?

I see neither the trail nor any markers. Not in any direction. Not for a quarter mile. The pressure builds, tight in my chest, sharp behind my eyes. Finally, I crack.

"Fuck it," I yell aloud, seething with rage, declaring my retreat. I grab my gear and set off in a huff, heading back the way I came.

I have no other choice. Anyone in my situation would have to do the same.

Deep down, I know it's not the truth. But in the intensity of the moment, I'm convinced.

I can feel my beat-up old 4Runner calling to me from miles away. The cranky heater blasting dry warmth on my face is a narcotic fantasy of relief. I practically salivate at the thought.

Fueled by frustration, I barrel recklessly down the winding mountain trail, aiming for the river. I recall a wide forest road following the course of the river that will take me out of here. It had taken me almost a full day to walk to my camp. I'm determined to cut that in half, even if it means run-walking the whole way, propelled by the intensity of my emotions.

By the time the adrenaline runs its course, I'm down the mountain and on the wide road by the river. It's still five full miles back to the trailhead. The familiarity of the road calms me slightly, but the weight of my sunken pride settles in. Defeat has never sat well with me. So, in my juvenile desperation, I scan for something, anything, that might numb the sting.

Within half an hour, I spot a forest ranger in a pickup truck. I flag him down and ask for a ride. Only my back aches, but I exaggerate and say I'm injured. I feel like a loser. But at this point, I don't care. The ranger, the gentleman that he is, agrees without question.

My pack and my body thump like dead weight in the back of his truck. I don't bother sitting up or trying to look composed. I lie down and let myself be carried, feeling dead inside as the mountains spit me out of their territory.

Back at the trailhead, this flicker of human kindness stirs something in me, and I feel a hint of revitalization. I offer my thanks, traverse the parking lot, and climb into my truck. I plop myself down on the driver's seat and sit frozen in a kind of stupor, idling blankly alongside the engine.

After a few minutes of this, I start to form thoughts. I contemplate how I'll spin this story for friends and family. How I'll protect my pride. But in my heart, I already know the truth: I entered the Colorado Rockies with stars in my eyes only to leave in less than twenty-four hours with my tail between my legs. This is a story I'll only be able to tell when I'm mature enough to be honest about my defeat.

I slump back into the cloth bucket seat, the heat blasting on my face. I'd hoped for relief, but all I feel is the cold sting of rejection.

I thought this was going to be a month-long odyssey, and I'm back in a day. What am I going to do now?

When I finally gather myself, I pull onto the nearest highway and decide to just head south and figure it out from there.

I need a more temperate, more forgiving land. One that can help rekindle my flame. And so I begin to wander towards an unknown destination. I don't know where I'm going or what I am looking for.

All I know is a fire had burned off a piece of me.

II: WANDERING

I was born a fire child in every sense, brought into the world under the thick, muggy heat of an August sun. Leo, the lion, was ruling the sky.

Even as a boy, I sensed the fire inside my body as something powerful, warm, and always pushing me forward. Years later, I'd learn that all three of my major astrological signs were fire. It showed not just in my temperament, marked by bright enthusiasm and fierce competitiveness, but in the way I burned to move, explore, and discover something intense to engage with.

My first pursuit was wrestling. It wasn't a choice so much as a requirement by my father. For better or worse, I was good at it. There was something incredibly visceral about stepping into the ring, locking eyes with another person, and battling. The movements were a balance of power and fluidity. When they synced, they felt both empowering and graceful.

Victory lifted me high. Defeat crushed me. Either way, it was more intense than anything I'd felt sitting at a desk at school. The pursuit of glory captivated my fire, while wrestling practice gave it a path to blaze.

When I wasn't training or competing, I'd slip into the woods that bordered the briny estuary down the street from our house in southern New Jersey. I'd spend hours chasing reptiles and amphibians, fascinated by their movements, their earthy colors, their cryptic geometric patterns. Turtles, frogs, snakes—especially snakes, which horrified my dad—drew me in like living glyphs of something ancient.

The pathless woods shaped me in a way different from wrestling and school. The forest provided a whole palette of feelings, which ranged from primal fear to pure joy. It stimulated my adventurous side and engaged my imagination like nothing else could. Walking down a quiet trail, taking in the rich colors and musky scent of the forest, feeling the thrill of not knowing what lay ahead—that was what kept me grounded, happy, and passionate about life. It kept me a few octaves above the pure anger that often fueled my wrestling. And it fostered a budding love of nature's power, mystery, and beauty.

Even when I was indoors, I gravitated toward the elemental. I'd mix potions from beginner chemistry sets, watching powders fizz and colors change, captivated by the hidden forces at work. It wasn't the formulas that intrigued me but the sense of something invisible being revealed. In a world that felt so vast, these tiny experiments felt like magic I could touch. I couldn't explain why it mattered so much. I just knew I was witnessing something powerful and true.

The wordless call from nature became the first voice I ever truly trusted. Unlike wrestling, it was a pursuit that came purely from within. It didn't speak in sentences, but it guided me all the same. The clarity of the swiftly flowing creek made me feel clean inside. The triumphant songs of birds elevated my thoughts, brightening my spirit. The evening croak of the bullfrog would lull me into a trance, and eventually into a deep, peaceful sleep. I didn't know it then, but exploring that subtle, sacred, and inexplicable connection to nature would shape the rest of my life.

In tenth grade, I encountered the first words that truly resonated with the natural world I felt around me, in Hermann Hesse's *Siddhartha*. I hadn't expected much—school reading usually felt dull and heavy—but something clicked immediately. It didn't just tell a story. It asked questions about the nature of life and reality. They were the same questions I had already begun to wonder in silence, out among trees and creeks, long before I knew how to articulate them. *Siddhartha* opened me to the possibility that my quiet questioning wasn't a flaw, but an instinct.

The following year, in my eleventh-grade English class, I discovered I wasn't alone. Emerson, Thoreau, and Whitman echoed the same wisdom from *Siddhartha*, but in a more grounded way: that nature is not merely a backdrop to life, but a living source of enduring truth.

Still, despite my fascination with nature, I wasn't immune to the fraying edges of my teenage years. The world of expectations, social pressures, and hormones crept in like weeds, rooting into every open space. Like most others, I started stressing about trivial things: who my friends were, the clothes I wore, how I was perceived. By seventeen, my sun-bleached hair had darkened into a curly mess. I was restless and uncertain, standing at the edge of what felt like a black void, slowly realizing how hard it would be to avoid getting pulled into a world built for people interested in anything but nature.

I remember sitting at my cheap white particle-board desk in my childhood room, drafting a letter to *National Geographic*. More than anything, it was a plea: I didn't want to go to college. In addition to not fitting into society, I was also burnt out from the pressures of being an athlete. Thirteen years of wrestling had worn me thin. The rigor, the culture of domination, and the constant hunger all had started to hollow me out.

I dreamed of majestic mountains, gin-clear creeks, and the electrical vigor of being alone with the elements. I wanted to drink from the natural world, to let it take me on an epic adventure into the unknown.

I felt it like a flame in my guts: what I burned for could only be found outside, in the rarefied air of the high mountains. In my mind, they weren't just mountains but shrines, holding a mystery that called to me ceaselessly. And, in the way a puddle lures a child like a magnet, I couldn't resist nature's gravity. It was my obsession.

And still, despite having nothing tangible to offer society, let alone a company like *National Geographic,* I wrote to them anyway. I had to do something to initiate my adventure. But, what a fool I was. I was all passion, no skill. I didn't want a career. I wanted a portal, a way to step into the sacred unknown.

I remember pausing my writing to stare at my little shelf of turtle figurines shaped from clay, rock, or colored glass. My gaze locked onto a chunk of turquoise. It was probably fake, but the rich color opened something inside me, and I fell into a vision: I was soaring like an eagle through narrow sandstone canyons beneath a perfect turquoise sky.

I could feel the desert, the pull of the Southwest tugging on something primal inside me. From that vision, I knew in my bones: I didn't belong on the East Coast. I didn't belong in some polished institution of "higher learning."

But time passed, and my letter was never finished, let alone mailed. The cultural current pulled me along, and eventually, I did what was expected after high school: I enrolled in college.

My wrestling accomplishments earned me a scholarship and, more importantly, acceptance into a prestigious university my academic record alone wouldn't have justified. My parents were ecstatic. For a while, I basked in the glow of their pride, inflating myself from its warmth.

But the facade didn't last long. I couldn't shake the feeling that I was just playing a role in someone else's movie. It all felt so fake. I wanted to live my own script, not someone else's.

Within a month of my first semester, my sunny disposition dimmed into something closer to Holden Caulfield's from

Catcher in the Rye. Disillusioned, somber, skeptical of everything. In an effort to feel like myself again, I quickly began diverting my energy from complaining to plotting. Instead of partying, I spent all my free time dreaming of nature, reading field guides, and planning my escape.

Wrestling had always been my way to belong. It made me feel like I had a place, a purpose within society. But the inner inferno that once fueled me had dwindled to a flickering flame. Over the course of my first semester, my passion for wrestling achievements fully extinguished itself and I was left standing at a crucial juncture: either continue fantasizing about following my call to nature or take action.

After a few weeks of painful deliberation, I finally gave myself permission to try things my way. I did some research and found out I could take a "leave of absence" for at least a semester without consequence.

A few days later, I built up the courage to tell my family and my coach. My dad was flabbergasted. My coach told me I had so much potential and urged me to talk to a psychologist first, to be sure I wasn't making a mistake. My dad agreed. In my heart, I knew my potential lived off the wrestling mat. But to placate my coach and honor my father, I spoke to the psychologist.

To my surprise, he told me that it sounded like I needed to take some time to find myself. He affirmed that my plan was well thought-out, especially since the process of picking up where I left off at the university would be simple. His support allowed me to go through with the plan.

During the leave, I first moved back home, comforted by support from my mom and sister. I worked for a few months to buy supplies, and then hit the road with my sights set west, toward the Rockies.

The beginning of the trip is a blur. My truck broke down

in southern Virginia and again in rural Georgia. I spent long, chilly nights in the back of my 4Runner, eating peanut butter and reading by headlamp. I considered selling the truck altogether and walking the Appalachian Trail all the way to Maine. Then a rainstorm—one of those wild, emotional downpours that seemed to speak—triggered a fast decision to keep the truck and make a run for my grandparents' house in Arizona.

Somehow, I made it. I stayed with them for about a month, resting, recalibrating, and dreaming. The brown tones and sharp sunlight of the desert stimulated my mind, but eventually started to feel oppressive. I wandered through arroyos, climbed desert peaks, and quietly asked myself what I was really doing.

Eventually, I set my sights on the Colorado Trail. It promised something epic, something wild and worthy.

As I drove north, windows down, Tom Petty's *Runnin' Down a Dream* blasted from the stereo. The beauty of the sun setting over the canyons and mesas of northern New Mexico branded itself in my memory, along with a crystal-clear thought:

Where the desert meets the mountains. That's where I belong.

I sat with the thought. Let it settle. Then I pressed a little harder on the gas pedal and crossed into Colorado for the first time in my life.

✦ ✦ ✦

The bitter cold of the Colorado Trail is now in my rearview mirror. Deep and low, like the purr of a cat, the drone of my 4Runner's tires cruising down the highway soothes me. I blast through Kansas, still cold and rainy in the early spring season. Then, I dip down through Missouri to pick up Route 40 in eastern Arkansas.

I feel a palpable shift when I enter western Tennessee. The air is much heavier, allowing my body to relax into its comforting embrace. I finally feel like I've outrun the freezing snow.

The sky is filled with graying clouds, but the sun breaks through, bright and enthusiastic. I roll the windows down just enough to let in the pungent breath of spring. The warm air is tinged with riverbanks, distant fields, and a hint of the piercingly fresh scent of oncoming rain. Not a hint of snow is in the air, and I'm grateful for it.

I drive like that for hours, with the hum of the tires, the wind curling through the cabin, the steady pulse of a land older and softer than the one I just left behind. I don't know where I'm going, but it feels like more than drifting; it feels like remembering. Faint flickers of excitement start to build inside me once again. Like something important is just ahead, waiting to be found.

My mind begins to mirror the land. The adrenaline-fueled urgency of my escape fully fades, giving way to a more open, flowing state. As my 4Runner moves forward, so does my aware-ness, into quiet reflection. I think about the life I've lived so far, the paths I might take next. And, for the first time in a while, I start to really *see* the world that's in front of me again instead of racing through it.

Somewhere past Nashville, the landscape thickens with forest. The trees rise, dark and steady with limbs like silhouettes waving me inward, welcoming me into something verdant and alive. There's a warmth in the South I haven't felt in weeks, and it's not just the temperature.

I flip through radio stations and land on a single, spare melody: "Hurt," by Johnny Cash. The slow, haunting honesty in his gravelly voice cuts deep. The lyrics speak of illusion—about building a life that looks strong on the outside but feels empty within. Somehow, that truth hits harder than anything I've felt in days.

My foot eases off the gas. I let the pines rush past and the music carry me. I think about how much I've tried to prove my worth, how many miles I've run chasing a version of success that is so clearly not true to me anymore.

I'm not ready to go home. But I'm not chasing the same intense vision anymore, either. Something is softening. Shifting. Transforming. Not just in the environment, but in me.

Signs point toward a town eight miles away, so I continue onward. When I arrive, a few beat-up old buildings and a dingy-looking Walmart are all the town seems to offer. I pull into the Walmart and walk inside.

Secretly, I'm hoping for a little adventure. I imagine meeting a beautiful girl my age. She shows me a secret fishing spot and we spend the day laughing by the water. She sneaks me into her room that night, and, well, you know the rest. By morning, we're soulmates. I go back to college, but we write each other poetic letters. Eventually, we marry and settle into the charm of the South.

The spell breaks and I'm staring at a shelf full of SPAM and canned meat. I find a familiar can of tuna, stock up on peanut butter, and wander the aisles, still half-hoping she'll appear.

She doesn't. Of course she doesn't. Even if she had, I would've mumbled something awkward and blown it. I was way more confident on the wrestling mat than in the arena of eros, after all.

That night, I drive with the windows down and Metallica's "Wherever I May Roam" blasting from my speakers. Hetfield's voice growls over the rushing wind. His anthem of raw freedom becomes mine, and reminds me that wandering, though softer than conquering, doesn't mean failure. It may be the freedom I was truly seeking. Rooted in nature, unchained by expectation, and truly sovereign.

I follow my muse, which leads me down a back road and into a woodsy neighborhood. A picturesque white house up on a distant hill catches my eye. As I drive toward it, I spot a little creek on the side of the road. I park in a tight pull-off and get a closer look.

To my surprise, the water is crystal clear. I was expecting murk, like the slow-moving, sediment-rich streams back east. But this stream is different. Tiny. Shallow. Barely significant in size, but somehow, captivating. Gentle angles and mineral staining are etched, like abstract art, into the brown slabs of stone from years of water gliding through.

I crouch beside the stream, out of both curiosity and reverence. The water shimmers with soft light, which becomes a translucent flowing chalkboard for the mathematical equations my mind begins to trace. Symbols superimpose themselves on the water's flow and then disappear into the current.

Then nothing. Just movement. Just beauty. Something inexplicable, somehow recharging my fire in the raw truth of creation. Something timeless is speaking, and for a few quiet minutes, the water holds me in a trance. A snippet of truth emerges: Nature's regenerative power doesn't only live in the ground or in the wild. It lives wherever you are. Wherever you choose to notice it. Wherever you need it.

As the sun fades, I part ways with the creek and accept the fate of another night in the back of my SUV. I find an empty parking lot and tuck myself into a far corner. It's a clear, tranquil starry night. I should be able to sleep. But I keep sitting up, staring out the side window, half-hoping to see a circle of people forming around a bonfire in the nearby field. All I see are shadows.

For the first time on the trip, I feel lonely.

So much of my time on the road had been filled with imagination. I'd read philosophy, daydreamed, imagined photographs I'd taken on my adventure woven into some epic book I'd one day write. I envisioned myself returning home triumphant, mountain-weathered, sharp-eyed, and rugged. Those fantasies used to carry me to sleep.

But not tonight. Not after the anticlimax in Colorado.

I've taken some photos. I've written a poetic letter to a friend. But in the absence of a real story—a heroic journey—I feel hollow and afraid as the darkness of night penetrates me. That feeling follows me deep into the night.

Morning arrives. I awake to birdsong and warm light brushing my face. I sit up quickly, suddenly flooded with the surging vitality of a recharged body. Something about that little creek still lingers in me, as a quiet but unmistakable message: *You're in the right place.* Whatever self-pity and fear remain within me dissolves quickly in the sunlight.

I know I'm not ready to go home. It's time to try again.

I dig out my map, scanning for the green zones that designate state and national parks. My eyes land on a name just across the Kentucky border: Daniel Boone National Forest.

I lean closer, tracing the access roads with my finger. Two options. After a moment's pause, I choose the one that leads deepest into the wild.

I fold up the map, crawl into the driver's seat, and fire up the engine.

I head north.

III: INITIATION

Daniel Boone is remembered as a pioneer and explorer, a man who left behind the safety of settlements to live closer to the land. Over time, his image was mythologized, shaped by poets like Lord Byron into a symbol of rugged independence and frontier freedom.

Today, his thick-bearded face still evokes the archetype of the lone wanderer who turns from comfort in search of something raw, vital, and true. A stretch of forest in eastern Kentucky bears his name, running along the western edge of the Appalachians. Looking back, it's no surprise I was drawn to this landscape. It had the feel of something ancient and wise.

I pull into an overgrown parking lot and step outside. The forest glows deep jade green. A trail disappears into the trees. It's an enchanting scene, and I itch with anticipation in the gravel parking lot at the forest's edge.

This already feels different. Like a painting I've seen before. Like I'm being invited in.

Something about this place also feels vivid and uplifting, an inner confirmation of what the stream has told me: I am definitely in the right place.

Though I've never been anywhere near Kentucky before, the land also feels strangely familiar. The soft moss, the scattered carpets of grass, and the rounded hills are a far cry from Colorado's sharp, alpine austerity. The air is moist and fragrant with earth. It smells of life. It also smells like home, similar to the northeastern woods where I'd wandered as a kid, searching for snakes, crouching near creeks.

The sun warms my back. The ground radiates its heat upward. My body softens and my movements become elastic and smooth.

I hoist my pack and step into the trees with a confident and steady stride. The trail is an overgrown double-track bordered by clover, dark soil, and soft gray gravel. To my right, a sandy stream sings its quiet song. It's just enough of a beat to sync the rhythm of my walk to.

My spirit lifts even higher. Time slips by effortlessly. It feels as if I've walked through a portal. Behind me lies the frozen silence of Colorado. Ahead, something altogether different. Something dreamlike.

I didn't need to be a hero. I just needed to get out into nature and find the right place.

Often, in more familiar terrain like this, I'd be fantasizing about somewhere more extreme. Glacier-capped peaks, turquoise mineral lakes, sheer rock faces. But something has shifted. It's as if my will had to be broken in order for me to receive something in this place. Something softer.

I had to fall to find the door. And now that I've stepped through it, everything feels more alive. More surreal. Like the fairytales I'd read as a child. Except I'm on my own now, walking.

I feel a buoyancy in my chest as I follow the trail deeper into the woods. No heaviness, no urgency. Just a quiet joy rising from within, warm and steady. The air smells rich with damp earth and leaf rot, and every few paces I catch a new scent: ferns, clay, something floral. The trail gently weaves through the forest like it's laying a path just for me.

I pass a few small caves carved into the hillside and duck inside them, poking around like a kid hunting for treasure. Back on the path, I slow even more, noticing the soft green shimmer of moss beaded with dew, the rough dryness of tree bark under my fingers. My arms swing loose. My senses feel bright. Every step is easy. Every detail is alive.

Ahead, I see a strange shimmer of color on the trail, like sunlight caught in motion. As I approach, the movement takes form: a living carpet of butterflies, slowly pulsing their wings in rhythm with the forest's breath.

I approach steadily, not wanting to disturb them. Yellow and black Tiger Swallowtails open and close their wings like stained-glass fans. Red-Spotted Purples flicker with flashes of amethyst and ember. Dozens more flutter around me in slow spirals.

The scene disorients me a bit. All I can think is: *What's going on here? Is this even real?*

I drop to my hands and knees on the sandy bank. Something shifts: My thoughts go quiet, like they've been soaked up by the thrum of the forest. The boundaries of my body begin to blur—not suddenly but a slow softening, like fog melting into water. The ground doesn't feel like a surface anymore. It feels like a skin I share with the world.

I feel like pure electrical energy. I'm still anchored, but lighter, less attached to the usual weight of my body. In my mind, I'm suddenly much younger, maybe four or five years old, and I am pure awareness, unencumbered by anything except the rapture of witnessing what's in front of me. I'm in a pure state of some kind, more hazy and dreamlike in my lucidity.

For a moment, I'm not watching the butterflies. I'm flying with them.

I wouldn't have called it anything then. I wouldn't have dared to try to use words to capture it. But looking back, it was a kind of quiet baptism; an entry point into the deeper layers of the land, and thus myself. A soft initiation down a hidden trail I hadn't known was there.

I stand up. The dreamlike state begins to fade. *That was strange.* I ignore the thought and start walking again, carrying the butterflies' quiet presence like a lingering scent.

I notice a larger river about six feet wide up ahead and everything snaps back into sharper focus. My pulse quickens at the sight, and a bolt of exhilaration sends some extra power into my step. I find myself running, then accelerating into a full-on sprint toward the uneven mossy riverbank. I arrive at the edge and nearly fall in as soil and rock collapse into the chaotic, almost-clear water.

The clean, mineral-rich aroma of the river instantly fills my nostrils. Its presence resets my mind, tuning me into the realness of the land around me. The mystical vibes of my stroll are replaced by the urgency of the rushing water. And then a realization: I need to find a place to set up camp before the sunlight fades.

Okay, time to get practical.

I follow the river as it weaves its way through the bumpy hills and decomposing leaf litter carpeting the forest floor. In places where the river bends and cuts into a knob, a jagged, bluish-gray underbelly of stone is exposed. About half a mile from the trail, a few yards from the river and near one of these rocky knobs, I get a good feeling.

Here. I've arrived. My signal to set up camp.

The next four days pass uneventfully. Each night, I fall asleep to the hum of insects in my little orange one-man tent. Each morning, I wake to sunshine and birdsong, eat from my food stash, then wander the woods. In the afternoons, I fish for dinner, gather firewood, and then build a fire.

Between tasks, I bask in the sunlight near the river, drifting between the warmth of the forest and the waves of thought in my mind. I read Jack London's short stories, or, when I crave something more contemplative, dip into *Walden* or my battered book of Robert Frost poems.

Wake. Wander. Read. Fish. Sleep. Repeat.

It had been six mornings since I left my 4Runner and stepped into the Kentucky wilderness.

Then came the seventh.

It's still pitch dark—probably around 5 a.m.—when I'm jolted awake by a bizarre, prehistoric cry. It erupts from the tree directly above my tent. Loud. Piercing. The kind of sound that makes your eardrums vibrate and your brain rattle.

Then silence.

I curl deeper into my sleeping bag, trying to will myself back to sleep. A minute passes before it screams again, longer this time, more brutal. I press my palms against my ears.

Again, it screams. And again. And again.

Eventually, I snap. *What the hell is that thing? I'm going to kill this stupid creature.*

Fueled by blind rage, I explode out of the tent barefoot, half-naked, wild-eyed. I fumble around in the dark, hands sweeping the forest floor for something heavy. No rocks. Just a thick stick. Good enough.

I wait, tense, searching the branches above for movement. Nothing. Just shadows and pale moonlight. The cold settles on my skin. The wind brushes my bare body.

This is insane.

Mud clings to the soles of my feet, and I start to worry about getting the tent dirty. My anger cools into quiet humiliation.

I sit in the tent doorway, wipe off my feet, and slide back into the sleeping bag. Defeated, shivering, and slightly embarrassed. But slowly, the warmth of my own body returns. Sleep begins to take me.

And then another scream.

I press my hands into my face. *You've got to be kidding me.*

Desperate, I unzip the tent, grab the stick, and launch it into the sky. It cracks through branches and lands with a dull thud.

Silence. I crawl back into my bag, close my eyes…

And the creature screams again.

I burst out of the tent and shout an obscenity into the darkness, hoping to scare it off with my human voice. But nature doesn't flinch. By the time I crawl back into my tent, my feet are cold and gritty with damp earth again. The wet, dark, wild night presses in around me. But eventually, my body warms. My breath slows. I melt into sleep like a stone sinking into the muddy stream bed.

Just before dawn, the creature lets out one last cry and falls silent. I never see it. But I hear it fly off, like a shadow returning to the trees.

Finally. Now I can rest.

I sleep for maybe one more hour. That strange, wild cry I couldn't silence felt oddly fitting as I drift off, like the forest had finally spoken in its own raw, untamable voice. It is telling me: *It's time to go.*

When I unzip the tent, the forest is aglow. Everything that felt dull and irritating the night before is now touched by light. Edges softened, particles swirling in golden beams. The sun is low, casting long fingers across the riverbank. Every leaf seems to shimmer. I sit on the moss and let the light wash over me.

The river bubbles and speaks in a new voice. Not commanding. Not loud. Just… certain. The message now rings clear as day in my thoughts: *It's time to go home.*

And for the first time in a long while, whatever lies ahead feels good.

IV: BLUE FLAME

After I pack my gear into my bag, I set off in the direction of my 4Runner. The trail opens ahead, and there's a song playing in my mind. Not a sacred chant or a grand anthem but "Travelin' Soldier" by The Dixie Chicks. I sing along without thinking.

The softness of the song, the ache and humanity, fills me with something quiet and good. My steps fall into its rhythm.

My hunger for wilderness doesn't feel urgent anymore. It feels like something that will unfold over time, now more of a relationship than a rescue. And somehow, that brings peace. I start thinking about the simple things: Friends back home. Fishing. Sharing food. Real conversation. Hard work. I no longer feel like I need to figure it all out in one grand wilderness epic.

I just want to live well. To earn my strength. To build something that lasts.

I don't need to abandon the world to find meaning. I just need to live close to my truth. And as the trail carries me forward, something else begins to stir: not emotion but insight. More truths begin arriving, wave after wave. The fog lifts, and it's as if I'm seeing through wiser eyes.

Golden light threads through the canopy. Dust motes rise like spirits in the breeze. Leaves rustle in a voice too sacred for language. In a burst of clarity, I now understand: I need to go back to college. Not out of obligation but purpose.

There's something there I'm meant to learn.

Then, in my mind's eye, I catch a glimpse of the coming summer: working with my uncle in Pennsylvania, helping him build his log cabin. A deeper part of my education will be physical, learning to build shelter with my own hands in preparation for a home of my own someday.

And maybe learning won't just happen in classrooms. Maybe it can happen from the land, in the texture of wood, the rhythm of rivers, the patterns of light and life that have always called me home.

For the first time in my life, I'm making decisions not from pressure or rebelliousness, but from clarity—the quiet knowing that my inner compass is leading me somewhere. And that clarity isn't just a gift. It's the result of the choice to find it. A commitment to listen inwardly and look to nature, to trust in my inner drive even when it means summoning the courage to step away from expectations.

Beneath all that clarity, something warmer rises: A quiet, radiant joy. I close my eyes and see a blue flame dancing. And, in that moment, I realize that the very fire that had once burned me is now within, illuminating my truth.

I wouldn't find a way to articulate my "leave of absence" experience for years, but this is where nature began to teach me. This adventure was my initiation—by the land itself.

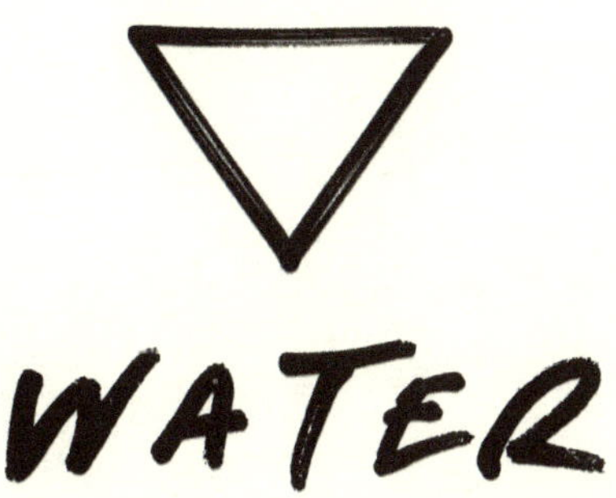

WATER

1: IMMERSION

I'M SITTING ON a narrow rock outcropping overlooking the roiling, muddy Rio Grande as it weaves its hefty mass toward Albuquerque.

Inside, I feel just as heavy, my thoughts swirling, emotions thick as mud. It's as if Poseidon himself has risen from the depths of my mind, dragging me into a silent wrestling match. A battle not for triumph but clarity.

I've come to this place to figure out how to navigate a pivotal life decision. A marriage is at stake. So is the happiness of several people, including my three-year-old son.

And yet, the sun warms my skin with golden indifference. The breeze combs gently through my hair. It's a perfect New Mexico fall day. The contrast is almost mocking, though I'm glad I'm here. If there's anywhere to sort out a mess, it's this place.

I lean back on my hands and let the gritty sandstone hold me. Below, the muddy river churns like a sleeping giant: slow but immense, the surface laced with foam and copper light. A crow circles overhead, emitting a distant, guttural cry. The scent of sage and sunbaked clay rises with the breeze.

Everything around me is spacious. Even though my mind is full of knots, the land is open and vast enough to hold the weight of it all. I close my eyes for a moment and try to slow my thoughts down, matching the rhythm of the river.

It works: As my inner storm calms a bit, I find myself reflecting on the steps that brought me to this moment. I think back to when I met Amy in my final semester of college in Virginia. I was working part-time at a gym to make some money, leveraging my years of experience in the weight room from cross-training as a wrestler. As graduation approached, I was dreaming of moving west to build a life in the Rockies.

I imagined working on a crew building log homes. I'd helped my uncle with his during several summer breaks, and I wanted to build one for myself someday. It felt like a path to both a steady income and the practical skills to shape a freer life. One that would bring me closer to nature.

Before Amy, I imagined myself living in a cheap shack in the mountains, fetching spring water, fishing cold rivers, and living in zen-like simplicity. I'd save every dollar for land and eventually build a house of my own. Then, I could work less, live more, and follow wherever my call to nature would lead me. I figured that once I lived more closely connected to nature, I'd convey my inspiration through poetry and philosophy, like Whitman or Thoreau.

Somewhere deep inside, I knew I not only had to find a special place to live, but I also had to learn something essential from the deep well of truth held within the land. I felt it to be personal—holding keys to my own truth—but also about something more universal and far beyond myself. Something that would become my work and help others as well. I trusted I'd find my way as I walked it.

But I found myself at a crossroads when I met Amy.

In the beginning, being with her was fun. Though we met at a gym, she also liked being in nature. She slowed me down a bit, preferring to just hang out by the water over exploring rugged mountain terrain. She was from a rural area, which made her seem softer compared to the career-driven personalities I'd known in college. She liked road trips, relaxing spa days, and lazy days by a lake.

As much as I craved solitude and adventure, my relationship with Amy scratched an itch for companionship. Deep down, I was a romantic. I longed to share my journey with someone. And I needed a person who would help me slow down and heal from my intense upbringing, which centered around achievement in sport. I thought I'd found that in Amy.

But I hadn't yet given enough weight to the importance of aligning well with a partner. Not just in shared interests and good vibes, but in higher dreams and visions. Amy's dreams were similar to mine on the surface, but in their essence, they diverged strongly. She was more socially-minded, drawn to community and belonging. Her soul was also pulled more toward the misty lakes and quaint, charming towns of New England. She was not naturally drawn to the mountainous, remote regions I was being pulled to in the Rockies.

Still, she was willing to come west, as long as we didn't live too remotely. Instead of a cabin in the forest, we'd settle near a small town. I figured this was the price of companionship. We'd start somewhere halfway between us, and hopefully be able to meet in the middle.

While we were researching towns and planning road trips, I started training hard again, this time in jiu jitsu and mixed martial arts instead of wrestling. Reverting to martial arts stroked my pride and gave my fire an outlet that, in the absence of the rugged lifestyle I craved, felt adventurous and thrilling. But something about it also felt like going backward, not just in time, but in my own evolution.

I knew, deep down, that I was fighting within myself. One part of me craved adventure. The other wanted what Amy wanted, a more "respectable" life that other people could understand, validate, and share. And provide financially. I was trying to make the two sides of myself shake hands. Going west with Amy was an attempt at marrying these opposing drives.

We found a small town in northern Idaho that seemed to fit. Together, we opened a fitness, yoga, and martial arts center, bringing our gym lifestyle from Virginia to the northern Rockies, in a town that was more lake than mountains but had both elements.

At first, we lived on a farm outside of town, which I loved. But slowly, we drifted closer to town. Eventually, we were living in an apartment above the gym. We were surrounded by a mountain paradise yet living like gym rats—literally inhabiting the ceiling of our gym—too consumed with business matters to really get out and explore.

Most of our energy went into running classes, managing the admin side of the business, and keeping up appearances by sculpting our bodies into picture-perfect shape. In many ways, it was a smoother path to success than the competitive martial arts lifestyle: less sweat, easier to maintain, easier to be praised for. It gave me a sense of control, of validation, even admiration.

But gym life wasn't satisfying my yearning for nature. It felt hollow, like I was chasing something easy and self-inflating instead of something true. It was a high that cost less but took more. Trying to survive in a small town economy also made each month a fight to stay afloat financially. And Amy wasn't fulfilled either. After three years of struggle, we let it go.

The Rockies had spit me out again.

We moved back to Virginia for a better opportunity. Then, after a short stint in Montana working at a guest ranch, Amy became pregnant. I had job offers in both Montana and Connecticut, but the pregnancy pulled her back east again to family, to security, to what she truly wanted.

It started to feel like some unseen current kept dragging me back east, no matter how hard I swam. After our son was born, the truth became harder to ignore. It wasn't just that the mountain dream was financially hard to sustain. I was also fighting Amy's dreams. Or maybe, more honestly, we were quietly fighting each other's.

11: REFLECTION

I blink and take a long breath, slightly disoriented from tumbling through a decade of memories. And I still feel no closer to clarity.

I rise and begin climbing across the sandstone formations, hoping movement might shake something loose. The textured rock grounds me, steady and warm beneath my hands. With each step, I feel more anchored in the moment and within my body. My anxiety softens.

I spot the river again and work my way down. My boots carve loose tracks in the dirt as I descend in a zigzag, stumbling toward the current. There's not much shoreline. Just a scraggly juniper tree clinging to the slope, its roots exposed and reaching toward the water.

Balancing on the tangle of roots, I gaze into the swirl. The river draws me in, and suddenly I'm somewhere else entirely: my college dorm room, maybe a year after my first Rocky Mountain quest and a few years before I met Amy. I'm sitting at my desk in the dark, playing the same song on my computer on repeat: "Losing My Religion" by R.E.M., the MTV Unplugged version.

The lyrics felt like a poem about me, feeling caught in a sticky, emotionally charged space. It prompted me to reflect on the decade and a half I spent pursuing wrestling. And woven within that, my relationship with my father.

A wave of memory rolls through me, my entire wrestling life, starting at age four. My dad, beaming when I won and sometimes withdrawn when I lost. His joy felt like my worth. His disappointment, my failure. I knew he just wanted me to become my best. But, the song told me what I didn't want to hear: It was time to let go of the sport. To lose my religion, so I could become something else. Something truer to myself.

But I wasn't ready. I held on. It took something stronger—a serious head injury—to force the decision. And then that injury introduced me to prescription pain pills.

I see myself lying in bed, floating in a narcotic haze. They made me feel warm, weightless, victorious. The sensation mirrored the high of winning. That startled me. Upon reflection, I realize that I wasn't just walking away from wrestling—I was still chasing the same feelings. Wholeness. Validation. Achievement. Only now it came through narcotics.

Even then, I knew the pills weren't what I truly needed, but they softened the landing. Gave me a hot air balloon to rise above the pain and emptiness I couldn't yet face. For a while, it was enough. But that high wore off, too. I saw what it was doing to my body and eventually quit.

I blink and return to the riverbank. The vision dissolves, but something in me feels cold and unsettled. A chill moves through my body, too familiar to ignore. It feels like withdrawal.

It's strange. I haven't touched pain pills in nearly a decade. I quit just before I met Amy, when the highs lost their warmth and my body started pushing back. I shifted gears. Started working out again. Became a personal trainer.

That's when I met her.

Looking back, I see the pattern in the current. I hadn't really stopped chasing the high. I'd just changed its source. From wrestling matches and my dad's approval to pills. From pills to sculpting my body. From working out alone to sharing that journey with Amy. But now even that high had worn thin.

So what high am I chasing now?

Another shiver, this one sharp and ghostly. Like a memory my body hadn't finished processing. I start back up the slope, hoping motion will warm me and clear the static. The shadows are lengthening. I want to feel the sun on my skin, in my bones.

With each step, something shifts. Every tremor feels like it's loosening an old layer. By the time I reach the top, I feel lighter.

I return to the same rock outcropping where I began. The sky is a lucid blue. A few clouds drift like thoughts I no longer need to chase. Just above the horizon, where earth meets sky, there's a glowing haze colored a soft magenta, almost surreal.

This doesn't feel like a landscape. It feels like a threshold between heaven and earth. No wonder the local painters reach for the desert palette.

Another memory rises. More recent this time: I see myself driving over the Beartooth Pass in western Montana, my dog Kona riding shotgun. The wind whips through the windows. The Rockies stretch around me like the echo of an ethereal dream. My chest is lit with joy. I feel free. Untethered. Fully alive.

I think of Steinbeck's line: *For all other states I have admiration. But with Montana, it's love.*

The memory of that moment surfaced for a reason. Something within me had risen to the surface.

III: PURIFICATION

The memory of Montana plays like a film in my mind's eye: I'm on a solo road trip while Amy is visiting her parents in New Hampshire. A few years after our son was born, we had moved from Connecticut to New Mexico to try to save our failing marriage. Taking a short break from each other was a last ditch effort to rekindle our connection.

I pull into a campground just beyond a dramatic pass, a few miles shy of the quaint town of Red Lodge. I'm still high from the surreal beauty of the Beartooths. Their light, their silence, the way the air felt impossibly pure. I drive slowly, scanning for a site near the river and spot one.

As I pull in, my eyes catch a woman across the way. Dark-haired, striking, close to my age. And she's alone.

I glance around, scanning for a companion. No one. A pulse of electricity surges through me. Somewhere deep down, I register a warning: *Uh oh*. But it's no match for the rush of excitement coursing through my body. I know I am treading in dangerous territory. Though we're on the rocks, I'm still committed to Amy.

I've come here for solitude. For clarity. Why is this happening?

The thought echoes in my head, but the feeling of excitement overrides the circuit. And part of me feels more alive for it. I'm far from the pressures of daily life. And in some twisted way, this feels like freedom. Like a pure, unfiltered expression of self.

The woman and I lock eyes. A small wave. Nothing more.

Now, I need to distract myself. I need to do something with the electric charge running through me. I park my truck, grab my fly rod, sling my tackle bag over my shoulder, and plunge into the woods heading toward Rock Creek. No trail, just following my instinct.

The trees reach like long, wiry fingers, brushing against my clothes as I duck and twist through the undergrowth. The excitement and elevation hit me all at once: I start to notice flashes of light in my periphery and a mild sense of unreality. Telltale signs of a migraine.

Is it a warning?

I press on. The sound of water finds me first. Then, there it is: Gin-clear water, gliding over freestone. One of my favorite phenomena in the world. The look, the feel, the smell, the sound. It stirs something deep within every time. I crouch at the edge, fingertips skimming the surface.

The headache symptoms vanish, just like that. Gone.

Strange, I think. That never happens. Once I notice the symptoms, the migraine is usually inevitable.

I rise, returning to the hunt. I scan the current for holding spots—soft eddies, underwater seams, the pockets where trout lie in wait. Upstream, near the far bank, I spot a promising configuration. I hone in on it. Everything else recedes.

Moving low, I work toward the target. Each step is slow and deliberate. The outside edge of the boot first, then a smooth roll to avoid sudden shifts in weight. Fallen logs, slick rocks, tangled roots—none of it breaks my focus.

In this heightened state I'm pure awareness again, like I was with the butterflies in Kentucky, but this time utterly locked in on my purpose. My senses are razor sharp; my body tunes itself fully to the task at hand.

Within range, I pause. Breathe.

I decide to fish the downstream edge first, approaching the trout from behind to give myself a clean shot. I strip a length of line and release the fly from its loop. It dances in the breeze.

I settle. I aim. *It's time to hunt.*

I glance behind me. All clear. If I angle my cast slightly over the river, I'll avoid snagging the trees at the edge of the riverbed. I raise the rod, feel it flex and load as I swing it back, then aim the line at my target as it swings forward. The line hums in the air. My little blue-winged olive lands a few inches off target though, a bit too far into the current. It skates past the eddy too fast. I strip in the line and cast again.

This one lands just right: Within seconds, a flash and a telltale splash of a fish biting. I set the hook.

Too slow.

The line jerks skyward, empty, and collapses behind me in a tangle of limbs and grass. I sigh and flick the rod forward without much care, hoping luck will lift the line. It doesn't. A dull tension pulls from somewhere behind me: A snag.

My heightened awareness lowers as frustration sets in. Ten

minutes of delicate tugging and untangling follow. I breathe slowly, trying not to let anger get the better of me. Eventually, the line comes free. I cast again, this time farther upstream along the seam where the eddy meets the current. I feed a little slack into the line to buy time on the drift. Nothing.

Another cast. Nothing.

I work the water methodically, each cast a quiet conversation with the river. Then I hone in on the top of the eddy just below a half-submerged log. It's a tight window, making it a tricky shot. But I get that quiet inner nudge. The kind I've learned to trust.

I cast. The fly catches the log.

I mutter under my breath, then smile. So much for the promise of action. I wade across to retrieve it by hand, soaking one boot in the process. I try a few more pockets before conceding that the fish aren't biting. The light is thinning. I head back toward camp.

The dream of fresh trout crackling over the fire is gone. But that's not exciting to me anymore. With no distractions left, my thoughts drift to the woman from the campground.

What exactly am I hunting now?

If I'm honest, it's not a new relationship. Neither love nor lasting connection. Just raw magnetism. Desire, and the ecstasy of dancing with it.

There's a part of me that wants to blame the marriage, to say I'm starved for novelty because I've been boxed in. But deeper than that is the innocent part of me that simply enjoys intensity. Something instinctual and raw. It's a desire I've spent years trying to bury. It's a hunger that doesn't ask for permission. It just wakes up and paces.

As I wind through the trees, my mind begins to shift. Rationalizations flicker like fireflies in the dusk: *I don't need to decide anything. I'm on vacation. I just need to feel alive.*

I don't allow myself to acknowledge I'm making a choice. Until it's clear I already have.

✦ ✦ ✦

The memories that begin to surface are surprisingly painful, sitting with the consequences of a decade-long relationship that's drowning.

It's hard not to feel the finger of blame pointed squarely at me. Maybe that's what this inner storm was trying to show me. And it's not just about Amy anymore. My son is part of this now. The weight of that settles like a stone in my chest.

I think about how easy it was to justify breaking the trust of our relationship. All it took was a convincing story. I'd think about the ways I felt mistreated or misunderstood and pile on reasons why I deserved relief.

Women just don't understand men's drives. So I just need to take care of myself.

There was always a rationale. But now, those justifications feel paper-thin. I let the full weight of my responsibility rise and settle. This wasn't a single moment. It was a pattern. And I can't hide from it anymore.

The shame crests and crashes. And beneath it, darker thoughts begin to swirl.

Maybe I am the reason. Maybe I'm just a lust-driven beast who never learned to tame himself. Amy seems to think that. And maybe she's right.

When I was ten years old, flipping through my parents' medical books, I felt a strange pull toward the drawings of the female body. It felt like the same thrill of an adventure into unknown territory. Was that the beginning? Did something awaken too early?

I'd hoped that being in a committed relationship would quiet the urges. But they didn't fade. They only grew louder. I tried to redirect them to be a good partner. But no matter what I did, they lingered, like some unkillable current beneath the surface.

Was it because I kept feeding them? Or am I just flawed?

It feels like there's no way to win. I either beat myself up for the desires or for the moments I've acted on them. Either way, I'm at war with myself.

I face the problem head-on, watching my own thoughts, asking for the truth. Eventually, the storm begins to ease. The thoughts don't vanish, but they slow. And in that space, a deeper voice surfaces.

It's not all your fault. Life is confusing. That's why you're here, figuring it out.

It's not an excuse. It's not denial. It's just a voice that feels beyond my own: clear, soft, and merciful.

A small warmth begins to build in my chest. Not pride. Not resolution. Just the beginnings of self-compassion. A flicker of light from somewhere deep inside, coaxing me onward. Not to escape from my mistakes, but to keep searching for something deeper.

I haven't found it yet. But I sense it's close.

The following morning, I pull out of the campground, and within minutes I'm cruising through downtown Red Lodge. It's another glorious, blue-sky Montana summer day.

Red Lodge is one of those western towns that makes you feel like you've stepped fifty years back in time. Main Street is lined with false-front buildings of brick and weathered wood. Restored vintage trucks and muscle cars fill the parking spaces. There's an aromatic mix of burnt motor oil, hot pavement, and crisp spruce needles in the air.

In my mind, I'm toggling between the memories of the night

before and the possibilities ahead. Now that the erotic energy is out of my system—at least for now, anyway—I feel ready to reconnect to nature. To reset. I want to find somewhere remote, far from people. I want to return to the heart of why I came to Montana in the first place.

I'm seeking the purity and truth of the wilderness, in hopes that I'll find some clarity about my relationship. I don't want anything or anyone pulling me off course again.

Once I'm past the edge of town, I pull off the highway and unfold my big paper map of Montana. My eyes trace the spine of the Beartooth Range as it sprawls westward toward Bozeman. A web of valleys opens between the shoulders of the mountains, some leading to high alpine lakes.

Normally, I favor rivers, but one lake in particular catches my eye. Maybe it's the shape. Maybe the distance from any main road. Or maybe it's just the name, Mystic Lake, and the fact that I'm in the mood for mysticism. Whatever the reason, I feel a pull: That's where I'm going.

I fold the map and ease back onto the road, the decision sinking in with a satisfying sense of purpose.

As I approach the valley, awe overtakes me. It feels like I've driven into a Bob Ross painting. The mountains loom in soft gray layers behind rolling green hills. Barns and silos sit nestled into the folds like they were formed along with the earth.

The road turns to gravel, and I catch my first glimpse of West Rosebud Creek. The water flows down from the lake high above. It's slightly tea-colored, dancing over rock and root. It looks "fishy," as we used to say when I was guiding in western Montana. My pulse picks up.

The hunt is back on. But this time, it feels cleaner. Truer.

This is the essence of what I'm seeking. The feelings from nature's beauty are somehow more pure—both primal and elevated at the same time.

I contemplate my conclusions, wondering if they are really true. *Is nature really purer than erotic desire?*

Then a thought bubbles within, as if answering my own question: *Maybe it isn't about purity. Maybe they are actually the same thing in different forms. Maybe it's just more about what you do with those feelings.*

I let that idea sit as I glide into the opening of the canyon, not letting the irony of the metaphor escape me.

The road narrows and climbs as it follows the creek. The forest thickens. The air smells cold and mineral-rich. I know the trailhead is at the end of the road, but I want to camp for the night before I get there. Somewhere quiet and tucked away.

On the left, I find a pine thicket with a few scattered campsites. It's mostly empty. Perfect.

I pull in and choose a spot close enough to the creek to hear its voice. I set up my tent and prep my fly rod, trying to stay calm. But my body is already buzzing.

I can't help it. Once my gear is ready, I take off at a near sprint. My steps feel light and powerful, like the earth is moving under me, not the other way around. When the creek comes into view, I slow down. Breathe. Take it in.

The water is glass-clear, tumbling over smooth granite boulders. The crisp, melodic beat of "Rain" by Blackmill echoes in my mind, syncing perfectly with the creek's rhythm. It fills me with radiant vitality, a feeling of youthful energy and pure innocence.

I cast my line. Almost instantly, a fish strikes hard.

It feels unreal, like a reward. I land it easily, slipping it into my net. I kneel on a granite slab and bow my head, listening to the smooth static hiss of the current, watching the water's dance, breathing in the wet, muddy perfume of the earth.

This is the essence. This is what I came to Montana for.

There's something about nature's presence and wholeness that brings out my own. I feel a current of pure, clean power pulsing through me. And, as I melt into a dynamic elemental dance so much older and greater than myself, I'm infused with a level of awareness far beyond thought. It's the raw, pure truth of creation, naked and ecstatic in its essence.

For a few moments, I almost fully dissolve into it. I'm a body crouched on stone…and I'm also everything. Creek. Cloud. Fish. Wind.

Then it fades. I come back to myself. My boundaries return. Thoughts resume.

But for a moment, once again, I was something greater than myself. And even now, a trace of that something still hums inside me.

I wake up the next morning feeling more refreshed than I have in a decade. I remember reading once that wild animals hold more "life force" than their domesticated counterparts. And that eating fresh game can transfer some of that vitality. All I know is that after falling asleep with a belly full of wild trout and the lullaby of the creek, every cell in my body feels fully charged.

Breaking down camp takes only a few minutes. I stow my gear, prep my daypack, and drive to the end of the road, where a small trailhead lot waits beneath the trees.

I lock up the truck, sling on my bag, and step onto the trail. It winds upward through forest, smoothed by thousands of footsteps but textured with roots and rocks. As I hike upwards, I am elated to be in such an enchanted place. The forest feels like my home, and I float through it as if drifting through a childhood memory.

Beyond the dam, spruce and fir stands carpet the slope. The scent of alpine trees and rich soil fills my lungs, and my breath feels like ecstasy instead of labor. I laugh, convinced it's some kind of happy gas.

The path turns to loose rock and begins to switchback up the mountain. After the final bend, it crests and winds back down toward the lake. When I catch my first glimpse of water, I stop in my tracks.

A long stretch of dark blue glimmers in the basin below, surrounded by towering cathedrals of immense jagged stone. The lake stretches deep into the peaks, disappearing into the distance. The lake reflects the clouds above it—both vast and out of reach—like a perfect postcard.

This isn't just mystical. It's majestic. But maybe those two ideas are really the same thing, too!

Apparently, in the altitude of Montana's mountains, my brain seems to be operating at a higher level, making connections I otherwise would probably fail to make anywhere else. In this place, everything seems to merge into one great clarity of mind.

I feel a rush of awe so full I can't imagine anything better than being alive in this moment. And the fact that I haven't seen another soul makes it feel even more vivid and imaginal. Far from the drone of society, and by contrast, more true in its elemental rawness.

After winding down the slope, I step off the trail and carefully pick my way down the gentle rocky grade towards the lake. I find the edge of what must be the lakebed during wetter seasons. I continue to the shoreline, crouch down, and slide my hand into the water.

Cold electricity races up my arm and settles in my chest. The coolness is the perfect counterbalance to the heat of the hike. I sit down, gazing across the lake. Then, I let my eyes drift upward.

My gaze follows the far mountainside and rises to a tall, leafless tree. From there, it jumps across ridgelines like stepping stones, finally landing on a patch of clouds hanging above the tallest visible peak.

Something stirs in me. At first, it's a soft, yet noticeable buzz in my spine. Then it grows stronger, like someone's turning up the volume on a frequency only my body can feel. My mind quiets. My chest warms.

Nature is so beautiful.

And in that moment, the clouds part. Light pours through and strikes me like a wave. I close my eyes as the brightness moves inward, pulsing through me, concentrating in my chest. It strengthens until it becomes an intense opening, a deep emotional outpouring that brings tears to my eyes and sends them streaming down my face.

The inner sensation continues to build and fills me with such immense joy I feel like I could float away. The feeling is both radiant and intimate, like a full-body prayer, releasing tightness and resistance from within my body and mind that I wasn't even aware I was holding. It feels like I'm having an orgasm in every cell of my being.

Then I hear it. Not with my ears, but from within: *This is your true path. Nature is your true path.*

The words come gently, but they carry palpable gravity, lodging themselves deep within. They aren't thoughts. More like pure signal flowing into me, coalescing into words, and etching themselves into my interiority. I don't analyze or argue. I don't need to. In this state, doubt simply doesn't exist.

The experience fades, and I'm still sitting at the lake's edge—quiet, buzzing, full of wonder. I stay motionless, unintentionally, because I don't know what to do. There's a stillness inside me deeper than silence. All the tension in my body feels like it's been wiped away. Or cleansed. I can't decide which.

I watch the wind brush the lake's surface. Light shifts across the granite peaks. And I'm just…there. Full of life, yet feeling empty and pure at the same time. I place a hand on my heart, half in gratitude, half to remind myself I'm still in a body.

It feels like something ancient has touched me, and now I'm carrying it within. I don't yet know how or what it means. I don't understand what just happened, but I know it was real.

And I know it matters.

I walk back down the trail, heart wide open. The joy stays with me, but part of my mind is already turning toward Amy.

How will I explain this?

The doubt returns, instantly dimming the brightness. By the time I reach the truck, the memory has already begun to soften. But the message hasn't left me.

I turn back toward the lake, place my hands together, and offer a small bow. Like I used to do at the end of martial arts class to honor my sensei. It feels right. I have the sense I'd just learned something profound from an ancient master.

"I will walk my true path," I whisper. "Or die trying."

IV: CLARITY

My awareness returns to the mesa in New Mexico. I'm back in the present, a few months after my Montana road trip, and ready to sort out my relationship with Amy.

And finally, I've found the resolution I came here seeking. Mystic Lake was the memory I needed. The message the land has been slowly coaxing me to remember.

The high I've been chasing all these years isn't about pleasure. It's not about escape. It's about alignment.

I've been seeking my true path—the only thing that brings me true power and real pleasure. The only way of being that shapes my raw desire into its fullest expression. The path doesn't kill or shame my lower desires. It gently coaxes them to reach toward something higher.

For me, that path is nature.

Only through nature can I water the seed of potential within, grow and cultivate myself, and ultimately bring forward the part of me that is most essential, most needed by the world. Other paths of desire might offer a temporary rush or release that makes the hardships of life more bearable. But if I walk them too long, they lead me somewhere that eventually begins to erode instead of build.

I've seen it happen. In myself. In others.

Any time I've compromised my path or let someone pull me away from it, I ended up seeking cheap highs, because I needed something to distract me, stimulate me, or release built up pressure. Drugs. Sex. Money. False purposes. Comforts. None of them are inherently wrong, but I was using them too often in lieu of my true high: exploring my connection to nature, my guide that reflects back the river of truth flowing inside me.

And I didn't see that clearly until I stood at the shore of that lake, pulsing with recognition.

In the light of that epiphany, another truth surfaces: The mistakes I made in my relationship with Amy weren't her fault. And they weren't entirely mine either. We both needed to fail to learn.

I needed to know the cost of living off-path. That cost was my health. My integrity. My ability to treat others and myself with the honesty we all deserve. My ability to focus. To stay aligned. To walk in truth.

I think back to that conversation with Amy after I returned from Mystic Lake. I told her something powerful had happened. I tried to describe it, but the words fell flat. My vagueness was met with frustration and doubt.

Understandable. She had her own truth. But I remember

realizing in that moment that our paths had diverged. That we weren't meant to walk together anymore.

Finally, I can see it clearly: It's time to end the relationship. Knowing this truth doesn't come with anger or finality. It comes like water after a long drought—soft, nourishing, undeniable.

My chest tightens, then slowly releases. I let out a breath I didn't know I was holding. And in its place, a deep stillness settles. Not peace, exactly. But clarity. And that's enough.

But then comes the harder question. The one that makes my heart ache: *What about my son?*

I think about the way his whole face lights up when he sees me. His laughter echoing off the bathroom tiles during bath time. The way he grabs my hand when we walk near water. He's already drawn to rivers. Maybe he already intuitively knows.

With that, deeper questions rise: *Which would serve him more? To have a father who sacrifices his path to stay close? Or a father who follows his path—and brings him along?*

I pause, letting that question settle in the silence.

My eyes wander across the mesa, and suddenly I begin to notice something I hadn't before: Paths. Everywhere. Faint trails worn into the dirt. The winding canyon below. The water's steady, unstoppable course.

Or maybe my higher self is using the land to show me what I already know.

A lizard darts across a sun-warmed stone and vanishes into a sagebrush. The canyon curves like a question mark, leading my eyes through layers of ochre and shadow.

The light here has a golden, forgiving texture. It wraps around the cliffs, playing upon their shifting shadows like a slow song. A song of time, etching its signature as a winding path of light and dark, layered rock and breathing sky.

I remember that I'm not alone out here, even if I'm the only human around. The land has been showing me this whole time. Showing me the way.

My true path isn't just something I blaze. It's something I listen and look for. Something I receive.

If I abandoned it, what kind of example would I be to my son?

I wouldn't want him to sacrifice his truth for anyone. Not even for me. So how could I justify doing that to myself, in his name?

I don't have every answer. But I know this:

I have to find a way to be in his life without making my own life a sacrifice. I have to live on my path, not away from it. Even if I have to swim against the current, like a salmon, I will find my way back to truth so I can flow forward with integrity.

That's the only way I can show up in life as the father he truly needs.

To abandon my true path would be to live a false life, inevitably full of seeking highs instead of truths. Nature had helped me find clarity amid a muddy situation and take the difficult first steps to get back on course.

EARTH

1: DESCENT

CAMERAS ARE ROLLING as concrete spews out from wooden forms I've erected for my stone cabin. Suspended over four feet above the ground, the concrete oozes out from stress fractures in the junctures between the forms, falling and smacking the dirt with a sickening thud.

I'm trying to appear calm, but the situation is rapidly unraveling. And millions of people are about to witness it on the Discovery Channel. The world is about to discover my incompetence, and all I can do is scratch my head and watch it happen.

The truck has stopped pouring, but the forms—now packed with tens of thousands of pounds of wet concrete and loose rock—are not only leaking, but visibly bulging, ready to blow.

The workers are glaring at me. One of them shakes his head in disgust. Under the crushing pressure, I break into a cold sweat. My calm exterior is cracking.

What the hell have I gotten myself into?

I'm over a hundred thousand dollars in debt. And now I realize I'm about to be buried alive. Not just by this project. By life itself.

This is going to end like my wrestling career: close, but not enough. Another second-place finish. A courageous, yet crushing loss. Maybe losing is my fate.

Seconds stretch like hours. The wet concrete continues pouring out of the forms steadily, forming large piles in several places. My breath turns shallow. I'm on the verge of full blown panic. The walls are literally closing in on me.

What am I going to do?

✦ ✦ ✦

After the breakup, Amy and my son moved to New Hampshire. I encouraged it. She needed the support of her family, and my son needed some kind of stability amid the turbulence. I cleaned up what was left of our life in New Mexico, packed my things, and made the long drive back East. Once again, I'd been kicked out of the Rockies.

I tried to reframe it as a chance to get to know the lush, hilly forests of New England. And maybe to finally return to the vision I'd held for so long: living in a cabin, close to the land, alone. What I didn't know was that, like in the myth of Hades and Persephone, my pull to the soil would lead me underground, into the shadowed world beneath.

Divorce meant financial pressure. I was the only one working. I had to get resourceful. At first, I crashed on a friend's pull-out couch in New York. Then I moved to Vermont and slept in my truck, trying to survive the brutal February cold. After that, I bounced between temporary housing arrangements, eventually landing a permaculture internship on a small homestead.

Even amid the instability, I felt something positive, like I was walking the edge of a clearer path. Permaculture's ethos of self-sufficiency and reverence for nature's patterns spoke directly to me. I was learning how to "think like nature," how to read the land and work with it.

The labor helped me reconnect with something primordial and good. The rhythm of a day's honest work, followed by early sleep, felt grounding in a way I hadn't felt in years. So simple. So direct. And I got along well with the farm's owner. We'd muse about the soul of the land, the inner shifts that mirrored our work pruning trees and shaping soil. But eventually, the internship ended. I had to leave the farm and move into a tiny apartment in downtown Montpelier. The shift from forest to town felt jarring, dissonant.

At the same time, I was adjusting to the new job I had landed just before the breakup. On paper, it was a dream gig: leading a company focused on nature-based fitness. The work centered on reclaiming our primal body, undoing the chair-bound stiffness of modern life. We taught people how to sit on the ground, rise without using their hands, and hold a deep squat. We balanced on logs, jumped across gaps, and climbed trees. I even traveled the world teaching workshops.

The lifestyle fed my hunger for freedom and movement. In many ways, it aligned with my values. And yet…something didn't fit. I knew that what I was seeking in nature went deeper than the physical. And whenever I gently introduced ideas about connecting more deeply with the land, I was met with disinterest. Deep down, I knew the further I followed the trail ahead, the wider the rift would grow between my job in society and my true path.

My relationship with women was also difficult to navigate. I wasn't grounded enough to approach a relationship in any way that extended beyond the physical. But intimacy so often seemed to stir up more hurt than ease. No matter how courteous and transparent I tried to be, many women wanted more. Some lashed out. I learned the hard way that for many people, crossing the bridge into physical intimacy was entering very emotional territory. And even when I thought I'd made my intentions clear and approached everything in a thoughtful, kind way, I still found myself tangled in messy situations.

The itch got scratched. But my desire seemed to keep me itchier than ever, no matter how hard I scratched it. I couldn't help but wonder: Why was I so itchy in the first place? I was more aligned with myself than ever, yet rarely comfortable. I knew it was pushing me to get out of limbo and find stability. What I needed was a calm place, free of distraction, where I could work, dream, and root deeper into my call to nature.

I knew I couldn't yet chase it out west, so I started looking for a remote cabin in Vermont. I needed to be near my son during his tender years. I wanted to offer him my presence and guidance. Vermont felt like a worthy place to try.

Each day after work, I'd drive to a park behind my apartment and hike up a steep, grassy hill to an old wooden pavilion. There, I'd unwrap a small cigar and take a few careful puffs. As the tobacco entered my bloodstream, a kind of meditative focus would set in. Energized but grounded, I'd start strategizing, mapping out possible paths to manifest my cabin dream.

Some days were hopeful. Most were frustrating. I wanted something off-grid, simple, and primitive. Something that would *require* me to apply what I'd learned through permaculture and resilience. But those kinds of properties didn't qualify for traditional loans. And, I didn't have a dime to spare, let alone enough to buy something outright.

I considered every angle but ran into roadblocks at each one. Every time I thought I'd found a viable lead, it fell apart. After a few months of this, I stopped trying so hard. I kept going to the pavilion, but I gave up planning. I'd sit and stare off into the pines, smoke curling around me, watching the sky shift above the treetops.

One day, I brought headphones. I opened Pandora and let it play whatever was queued. As I watched the fog roll through the pines, the song "Soul Meets Body" by Death Cab for Cutie came on. The lyrics cut through the stillness, lulling me into a meditative trance. One of the lines—*not one speck will remain*—landed with strange weight, reminding me of a conversation I'd had while personal training a friend of a friend in New York.

He was investing in a private off-grid compound in Maine and was interested in rocket mass heaters, which are efficient stoves that burn hot and clean by routing smoke through a long clay bench before it's released. The smoke is fully burned by the time it reaches the end of the chimney. No residue. Not one speck. Just like the song lyrics.

And just like that, a promising thought arrived: *Maybe he could help fund my project.*

That same week, coincidentally, a remote property appeared on Craigslist in the town where my permaculture mentor lived. Thirty acres of old partitioned homestead, backed by wild mountain wilderness in every direction. The name of the road is Jerusalem Hill, hinting to me that it would be a sacred spot. There was already a small shed on the property. I didn't know how I'd develop the land yet, but something about its photos spoke directly to my heart.

I gathered some more intel about the property then built a presentation, naming the project Sacred Acres. I superimposed a rustic timber-framed barn on a photo of the land and included a topographic map of the property. I wrote about my dream to build a cabin of stone and timber from the land. To create a permaculture teaching site. A place for workshops, connection, and stewardship. A place to grow a life aligned with the Earth.

I sent it to the investor. We spoke soon after. Green light.

I was elated. Energized. For the first time in a long time, it felt like everything was aligning. I wasn't just dreaming. I was building something real. But there was still one major obstacle in my path: I had to figure out how to build a house. Not only *what* to build but also *how*.

And also how to afford it. My investor had covered the land and left me a small cushion to get started, but it wasn't enough to fund the steep building costs. I had my heart set on constructing a cabin of stone, and luckily, there was ample stone scattered across the property. In my idealism, I figured I'd start with a trench, then lay the stone by hand—simple, elemental, the way I imagined our ancestors might have done it.

But my permaculture mentor quickly sobered me. He introduced me to the reality of frost heaving, a phenomenon where water in the ground freezes and expands, lifting anything above it, including stone and concrete. In Vermont, the frost line can reach four feet deep. With a shallower trench, the structure might shift and crack with the seasons.

If I wanted my dream cabin to last, I'd have to dig deep. That meant renting a heavy machine to cut through the rocky Vermont hillside. But to even *get* a machine on-site, I needed a proper driveway that was graded, graveled, and durable. The expenses stacked fast. No matter how hard I tried to stay optimistic, this was a big one. I racked my brain for creative solutions, but I couldn't make the math work. I was stuck.

Then, a week later, the answer arrived.

When I was in New York, my friend would often put on one of his favorite shows: *Building Off the Grid.* He'd suggested I should audition to be on the show, but that was before I had a project lined up. Now, with a project, I went to the show's social media page to see a casting call for the next season.

A hand-built stone cabin in the Vermont mountains was *perfect* for the show.

II: LABOR

I moved onto the property just as winter began loosening its grip on the mountains. It was mud season. My truck barely made it up the slick drive uphill to the old shed tucked in a pine grove on higher ground.

A few weeks earlier, my mentor had walked the land with me. His advice was simple: move into the shed and start by digging a spring. If I could tap into fresh, clean water, everything else would be easier.

At first, I camped beside the shed in my tent, waiting for the weather to warm and the ground to dry enough to start gutting the shed of old junk, rotten insulation, and whatever else was lurking in there. A neighbor mentioned that, years ago, this small, lofted shed had housed a family of three. That gave me hope: My dream was anchored in something real. If not yet comfortable, at least viable.

Bit by bit, and with the help of my son, I began to transform the space. We cleaned out the interior, tore out ragged insulation, and replaced rotting boards. Then we sealed the doorway and painted it blue, his favorite color.

It was rustic, but it was ours.

Some of our best moments were a short drive away, down by the White River. He'd splash in the shallows while I watched from the sandy shoreline, the late-day light catching the water's dance. To him, it was all adventure. Like camping but better. A way of life without excess but comfort in the purity of the elements. Just time, space, and the wild.

He carried a little blue Lego man everywhere. One day, it vanished somewhere in the woods. Each time he visited, he'd want to go searching for the "blue guy." It became a small quest, a symbol of his own budding relationship with the land.

I never had a fixed idea of what kind of father I'd be. I just knew I wanted to help him discover who he was and honor it. And the best way I knew to do that was to live my own truth. To let him see what it looked like to follow a path that felt alive, authentic, and rich in connection to the land. If I wanted him to believe in himself, I had to show him what that belief looked like in me.

And so we built—me with my hands, him with his silliness and presence. These weren't just bonding moments. They were the cornerstones of a larger vision. I wasn't only shaping a life for myself. I was rooting something deeper for both of us.

When he wasn't with me, I kept going. I mixed concrete in a wheelbarrow and built a simple casing for the spring. Then I hiked uphill about a hundred yards and began to dig. I struck water just a few feet down. It wasn't much, but it was clean, cold, and enough for drinking. I added a basic solar kit and carved trenches through the rocky soil with a pickaxe to bury internet lines. Primitive though it was, I was slowly building the infrastructure of a real life.

Each day, I'd drive down the steep, shaded road to the river. I'd strip down and bathe in its liquid crystal waters, the cold soothing my sore muscles, shocking my mind out of work mode and back into the beauty of the flowing present moment. It became a ritual of pure rapture, a sacred punctuation mark at the end of each day.

As the warmth of late spring pressed in, I felt strong again. My body was lean and agile. My mind was steady. The dream that had once existed only in scattered sketches and smoky visions was beginning to take shape, not just in my imagination, but in soil, stone, and sweat. Each step reinforced my trust in my path and the decisions I had made to get me to this place.

Higher up on Sacred Acres, I chose a homesite. The contours of the fields, forest, and hillscape seemed to cradle something unseen, like the land itself wanted to hold what I was building. It was elevated, well-drained, and already cleared of trees. My mentor agreed it was a strong spot. He came out to do the trench work, and I spent hours afterward sitting among the deep cuts he'd made, tracing blue veins of bedrock with my eyes. I'd stretch out on the raw earthen pad that stood in the center of the trenches and dream of my future house, letting the vision settle more deeply into my bones.

Soon, the driveway was underway. A dump truck rolled up and unloaded thousands of pounds of gravel onto the quarter-mile path I'd mapped through the woods. Then my neighbor, a third-generation Vermonter, brought his bulldozer in to shape it. When it was done, we filled in the foundation trenches with rubble, and I tamped everything down. It was slow, hard work. But it was honest. And every stone I set felt like a beat in a song I was finally learning how to play.

✦ ✦ ✦

I'm shoveling stone into a wheelbarrow, caught in a trance of rhythm and stillness. Dust swirls gently around, curling upward like incense. I feel joyful and triumphant in my labor. I swear to myself I could do this kind of work more or less forever. Sweat pours from my skin, salty and alive, and mineral grit from the stone slides into my pores, blurring the boundary between self and nature. As the wheelbarrow fills, something inside me empties. My selfhood nearly vanishes and I recognize this mode of pure awareness I keep finding myself in. My body toils, air heaving in and out of my lungs, oxygen buzzing in my bloodstream, and I wonder:

Is the barrier between me and nature even real?

This is the kind of experience I came here for. I knew that to move forward on my path, I had to go downward, back in time. Older tools. Older rhythms. Not to stay but to remember. To firmly anchor ancient memories into my overly modernized mind. And to keep my feet planted on the ground firmly enough to shape my fire into my highest possible purpose.

In the modern mind, time stretches forward like an abstract line, forward and backward against a blank background. But Earth knows better. Here, time lives in depth, not distance. It coils in bark and stone and the rhythmic breath of labor. In nature, building with my hands, I'm not escaping the future. I'm touching the memory of how humans first began to experience the Earth, participate in its rhythms, and shape it.

I know I'm meant to build this house. And I also know I'll leave it behind. Like the master who tells the seeker to build a shelter only to tear it down, I sense that the act itself, not the outcome, is the lesson I need right now.

I know this because there's a deep tickle inside me, already asking for something more.

Despite these wonderful experiences I keep having, I feel the sharp edge of a deeper hunger growing. One that can no longer be satisfied by fleeting highs and flowery thoughts. Or even solitude and a quaint cabin in the woods.

First off, I can't summon these states at will. They come like gifts and vanish just as suddenly. I know if I want to keep learning, I have to ask nature for more. I have set my aim toward a fuller descent. A deeper penetration. Not just into the experience of nature's power, but into the source of it.

I need to follow the arrow of time deeper into the land, and all the way to the soul of nature.

✦ ✦ ✦

At night, I'd lie on my mattress, a thin Thai pad laid directly on the bare wooden floorboards, and read. Just before the last light dimmed and sleep took over, I'd reach for anything that might offer a glimpse of this deeper truth I was after.

I sought out books that explored the connection between nature and spirit. Stories of others who had found truth and meaning through the land. I began with the works of Tom Brown Jr., especially his writings on tracking and awareness. Then came David Abram's *The Spell of the Sensuous*, a book that offered a more intellectual yet poetic angle. Others followed: voices from Indigenous elders, mystics, and theologians. Any arrow that pointed toward the soul of the Earth, I followed.

But I wasn't content to only read. I wanted to test it all in my body. I'd kneel in stillness, counting each breath. Stare into the blackness of my closed eyes, sometimes catching glimpses of geometric patterns forming and coalescing into a bird or but-terfly flapping its wings. Stretch into the shapes of yoga. Walk slowly through the trees with a softened gaze, trying to dissolve the boundaries of perception.

Could the Earth respond to my query? Could I tune my body to its rhythm well enough to hear? I didn't want just mental constructs of reality. I wanted contact. I wanted truth I could not only feel, but see, touch, and speak with.

My time to seek and explore began to dwindle. The cabin deadline loomed, winter crept closer, and I had barely laid four feet of stone. The producers of the show were growing restless. Emails turned to calls. Pressure mounted.

Thankfully, I wasn't alone. The fertile soil of Vermont had nourished more than my dreams and my bond with my son. It had also deepened my connection to people. Community began to take shape around the project. My early calls for help were answered.

A whole family from New York started driving up on week-ends, trading city schedules for wheelbarrows and sweat. A couple from Pennsylvania returned again and again. My friend from New York ventured up a few times and proposed to his partner beside the river in a quaint spot around the bend from the area I bathed each evening. A friend I'd met years earlier in China pitched a tent in the forest and stayed for months, mixing concrete by day and talking philosophy by the evening fire.

The cabin was no longer just a building. It had become a shared vision, an unfolding tapestry of story—stone by stone, soul by soul. What had begun as a solo mission was transforming into something more collective. Something rooted not only in Earth, but in friendship, in effort, in spirit.

For me, the cabin was never just a structure. It was a land-mark between my old life and the one I was forging through the land. It was the dream that had followed me since early adulthood coming to fruition. In the pressure-cooked halls of school, in the endless grind of wrestling, in the weight of relationships, I had always envisioned a simpler, more pure life. A place where I could be closer to the Earth, where the air felt cleaner, the demands quieter and more pure. Peace. That was at least part of the dream.

I didn't need it to be a masterpiece. I wasn't building for legacy or validation. I wanted to fully touch the ground, to shape something that felt like an extension of the perfection already present in the land.

Stonework wasn't my craft, but I came to love it for its weight, its permanence, its quiet authority. The design followed the principle of permaculture: Work with the land, not against it. It felt less like imposing my design and more like listening to what the land wanted. Collaborating. This was the first of my dreams that felt like it had roots.

The labor carved me. I wasn't just building with Earth; I was letting Earth rebuild me. By late-summer, my body looked like I'd been chiseled from the land itself. But even then, I could feel something was off. I was burning too hot trying to meet the deadline. I wasn't tending my fire carefully. I was feeding it everything I had, and then dousing myself in caffeine anytime it would dwindle. And it still wasn't enough for the timeline of the show. Despite peak effort, my plan began to fall apart.

It started with the concrete truck incident. The producer, eager to see progress, had hired the truck to accelerate the build. But I wasn't ready. The forms I'd constructed weren't adequately braced. As hundreds of pounds of concrete poured in, the pressure was too much. They started to blow.

For a moment, I stood frozen, watching my dream collapse in real time. But then, like a miracle wrapped in a grimy sweat-shirt and toothless grin, a senior member of the concrete crew jumped in. He scoured the site, gathering every piece of spare lumber and rebar he could find. With calm urgency, he braced the structure just enough to let the concrete begin to set. He saved the build, and maybe even the episode.

Then came the timber frame dispute. What was supposed to be a three-day job turned into a stalled, half-complete skeleton. I'd misjudged how many people I needed. I hadn't recruited enough hands, and the time investment on his part stretched longer than we expected. Money I didn't have became a point of contention. Understandable, but I was left stranded and out of options.

The final blow came when winter arrived early.

One day, the stone structure stood strong, akin to a fortress, proudly holding shape among the flaming golds and reds of autumn. The next morning, it was locked in frost. Totally encased in ice. The whole project went from looking noble to abandoned.

I didn't give up easily. Every morning, I listened to Jocko Willink's gritty drill sergeant voice, speaking about how discipline is required to achieve anything worthwhile. The words thundered in my chest like marching boots. No shortcuts. No hacks. Just hard work. Blood, sweat, repetition. The old-school grind. He's a Virgo, and thus, a voice of the Earth. I believed in the message. I believed in myself.

But belief didn't matter to the freezing mud. Or to the ice encasing my tools. Or to the stone that wouldn't move. No matter how many angles I tried, how early I woke, how long I pushed, I couldn't force the vision into being. And slowly, the part of me that thought I could grind through anything began to wear thin.

I'd been here before though: Years ago, my truck hit black ice and went into a tailspin. I tried to take back control, but that only made things worse. So I let go of the wheel, praying I wouldn't crash too hard. Seconds later, the snowy banks that lined the road softly caught me.

That was the lesson then, and it was the lesson now. Let go. Not only as surrender. But as wisdom.

The Earth wasn't yielding, and it was overpowering me. So, finally, I listened. No big revelation. No mystic light. Just the clear, hard truth that I was wasting my life force pushing against a brick wall. Time to regroup. Adapt. Flow around the obstacle like water finds its way through stone.

I cut a deal with the producers. They'd wait for the opportunity to throw up a "Hollywood roof" to make it appear finished for the camera. And that would be it. The illusion would be complete. The next day they would take it down, with the wood as payment for the carpenter who built it.

I filmed the final episode sick, exhausted, and defeated. After all that work, I was left with nothing. No roof for the cabin, no money to finish it, no warmth to weather the winter. The little shed I'd poured myself into was no match for the coming cold.

And just like that, I was homeless again.

Fortunately, I already had a plan in place. One night by the campfire, my friend RJ and I had cooked up a bold idea: We would host a movement retreat deep in the Colombian jungle. "RJ" stood for Recon John, a name he had earned during his time in the military. True to his name, he'd already gone ahead, found a retreat center, and sent word that it was the real deal—quiet, lush, and far from the brutal elements of Vermont.

I was still sick, barely functioning, but I booked the ticket anyway. It was a leap of pure faith. All I knew is warmth lay ahead.

What I didn't know was that I wasn't heading for refuge. I was headed for another descent, deep into the heart of the jungled Earth. Deeper into myself.

III: UNDERWORLD

I'm walking with RJ down a rocky, earthen road that winds through the lush Colombian jungle. We pass several beautiful *fincas*, the Spanish word for farm. The vivid green grass, the wave-like texture of the hills, and the intricate patterns of streams carving through the meadows create a scene so captivating it feels like a dream. It's an exotic, otherworldly place. I'm grounded only by the heavy musk of horse manure and stone beneath my feet.

Back in Vermont, RJ had called me with updates from his Colombia reconnaissance trip. It didn't take him long to find a nature retreat center tucked deep in a river valley, a few hours from the sprawling city of Medellín. A month later, just as he was about to fly home, he called again.

"I canceled my flight. I'm staying," he said. "I rented a house down the road from the retreat center. Oh, and I met a girl doing acroyoga. She moved in." I wasn't surprised. RJ never moved slowly.

On our next call, just before I flew down, he told me about an encounter with a local shaman named Juan, who lives on a permaculture farm. Juan had given him all kinds of powders and pastes to try and invited him to work with *yagé*, the Colombian name for *ayahuasca*—the powerful South American brew known for inducing hallucinogenic states. It was awesome, RJ said.

RJ wasn't new to plant medicine. As a war veteran, he'd spent years seeking ways to process his experiences, heal, and find his way. He'd worked with ayahuasca many times prior to this trip. So, knowing RJ, it didn't surprise me that he'd already found his way to a medicine man.

Now we're headed to Juan's place. Based on RJ's story, I picture a wiry, eccentric character, probably casual, eager to share plants as a kind of universal language. I'm open to the mellow medicines but not *yagé*.

We veer off the road and onto what looks like an overgrown drainage ditch. We duck through brush until we reach the river. The crossing is tricky, all slick stones and shifting footing. More than once, I nearly roll my ankle. On the other side, we step over a barbed wire fence and land on a narrow, grassy trail. Sharp stings light up my feet from ants, biting deep. Even in this soft, stunning place, nature has teeth.

Across the river, the landscape transforms entirely. While the dense jungle clings to the mountains in the distance, the immediate surroundings evoke images of Ireland—vast expanses of grass and fields carpeting bold, geometric ridgelines with boulder formations reminiscent of ancient castle ruins. Tiny creeks with butterflies circling lazily above them meander toward the river below.

We follow the path up a ridge. At the top, the land levels out. Just beyond a small pond, up a steep hill and to the right, stands an extraordinary tree. Its gigantic architecture, with limbs that spiral and flow like water, stops me in my tracks. Exposed roots curve out from the sloped hillside like arms, inviting us to come explore. I've never seen a tree so magical.

In the shadow of the tree, just past the pond, we pass a primitive bamboo structure. A fire pit sits at the center, and hammocks hang in all directions like a loose web. We follow a garden-lined path toward a simple white house with a small porch.

On the far edge of the porch, a man is seated, dressed head to toe in white. His hat is cone-shaped, like the kind fairytale gnomes might wear. His face is youthful, but his expression is serious. He hasn't looked up once, yet I know he's aware of us. His focus is absolute. He's licking something that looks like a lollipop and rubbing it in slow spirals against a wooden cone.

I'm caught off guard. This isn't casual. Not at all what I

expected. But I should've known better. RJ makes everything sound casual. My stomach tightens. I feel suddenly out of place in my tight tank top, arms out, ego loud.

RJ motions for me to take a seat on the bench near the door and sits beside me. We wait in silence, both gazing out at the view. After a few minutes, without looking up, Juan murmurs something softly in Spanish. RJ rises and walks over to him. They exchange a few quiet words. Then RJ turns and calls me over.

It's clear Juan doesn't speak any English. RJ introduces me in Spanish. I offer a soft bow and say, *"Mucho gusto,"* one of the few phrases I've retained from six years of classes. Juan looks up at me for the first time. His eyes are soft despite his serious expression. He glances at RJ and they exchange a few more words.

"He wants to know what you're seeking," RJ says.

The knot in my stomach tightens. "Tell him I seek to understand the connection between nature and spirit," I say. "And that I'd love to hear his worldview. Whatever he feels called to share."

Juan's gaze softens the moment the words leave my mouth, as if he somehow understood me without translation. My stomach loosens. After RJ translates, Juan responds. His voice is like a warm, slow song. The air seems to change.

He pulls out a bag and begins to search through it. RJ gestures for me to sit again. Juan produces a small glass jar filled with a black substance, followed by another with green powder. He opens the first jar, scoops out a small amount, and reaches for RJ's arm. RJ holds it out, palm up, wrist exposed. Juan wipes the black goo onto the underside of his wrist.

Then he reaches for me. I follow suit.

RJ explains that this is *ambil*, a thick paste made from tobacco. Juan says something, and RJ adds, "Juan says it's the Father."

RJ uses his finger to transfer the paste from his wrist to the inside of his cheek. He nods at me, and I do the same.

Within seconds, I feel its effects: grounding, sharpening, energizing.

As Juan begins to speak, RJ translates his words: "The force of creation is the Father. It started from nothing, but it was always there. Concentration created all that is. From it came water, the Mother. And then the Son. All are the Father."

He pauses.

Then, slowly, he picks up the jar of green powder. He uses a small wooden spoon to scoop some and reaches toward RJ, who receives it in his palm. RJ explains that this is *coca*.

I watch as RJ places the powder in his mouth and presses it into the other cheek with his tongue. When Juan places the second scoop of powder into my palm, I do the same.

Juan continues: "This is the Mother. It's so important to honor women. Always honor your mother, the Earth, and all women. They will nurture your heart. Honor the womb and the breast. Honor the sacred ground. And honor the feminine within yourself. These are the seeds of the creative force."

As the warm, euphoric buzz of the *coca* settles in, I feel something open. And I think to myself: *I'm in the right place. This is exactly what I was looking for, even though I had no idea I was searching for it here.*

Juan continues: "Live through your heart and nothing else. All other paths lead to destruction. The mind doesn't know the way. Only the heart knows. Without its guidance, we are lost. With it, we are found."

Then he looks directly at me. His gaze sharpens, not unkind, but charged with purpose.

"There are things we are not able to know," he says. "But by looking deeply within, we begin to see the forms of the world… then the planets… then the cosmos. Look within. Sit in silence for years, and you will see the truth of nature."

He adds, "All things in nature are born out of love. And that love is a teacher."

He pauses. Looks up, as if listening. Then, turning back to us with a subtle smile, he finishes:

"When we are enlightened, all of life tastes sweet."

He falls silent and picks up his wooden cone, returning to his meditative task. The weight of his words linger in the air.

After a few minutes, RJ breaks the silence and speaks to Juan in Spanish. I don't catch what he says, but Juan responds gently: "I offer these sacred plants to you as a welcome, like a handshake. And as an invitation, if you would like to go deeper. If you wish to work with *yagé*, we will plan for it."

I contemplate his offer. Then I ask RJ to translate: "Tell him I'm not interested in taking *yagé*. I want to help share the wisdom of nature—the way he speaks of it—but I don't want people to think they have to take something so strong to access it. I need to model that. I hope to write a book."

As I say it, doubt creeps in. *Am I being arrogant? Too good or pure to humble myself to the medicine?*

After RJ translates, Juan nods thoughtfully.

"If you don't wish to point others to the medicine," he says, "then you must become the medicine. That way, what you write will shine like gold."

He meets my gaze. "I wish you luck in your journey."

I nod, taking in the gravity of his words. RJ and Juan continue speaking in Spanish for a while. Then RJ turns to me.

"Are you sure you don't want to take it?" he asks. "We wouldn't do it for another week or so. Do you want to think about it?"

"Sure," I say. "I'll think about it."

With that, we say our goodbyes and make our way home.

Later, I take a shower—cold, the only option—and collapse

into bed. My gaze drifts across the etched red cinder block walls as jungle sounds fill the night air.

My mind returns to the afternoon. Everything about the experience resonated in an unexpected way. The landscape. The tree. The medicines. Juan and his words. The only thing that felt out of place was…me. Or more accurately, my mindset.

Why am I so against taking yagé?

It's not like I never considered it. When I was younger, I used to fantasize about taking peyote, imagining shimmering, colorful visions in the desert, surrounded by Native Americans beneath a starlit sky.

The truth is simple: I'm afraid of ayahuasca.

The stories I've read online talk about vomiting, ego death, and contact with spirits. I hate feeling sick. I'm terrified of losing my body… and especially of the idea of not being able to find my way back. And I don't want to meet spirits, especially not the dark ones.

I'm drawn to the truths of nature. This world. I'm not trying to travel to other dimensions. That's for the psychonauts. Not me.

But something inside me won't let it go. A voice inside reminds me of a principle I've lived by for years: "Jack of all trades, master of none." It's how I connect seemingly unrelated ideas and skills. It's how I learn. How I integrate. To understand anything complex, I have to look at many angles. Even when the connection isn't yet clear.

And then it hits me: *Plant medicine is nature. This isn't a synthetic chemical experiment. It's earth wisdom. Rooted in tradition. In soil and spirit. Just like the peyote I once romanticized.*

I picture the setting again: A campfire in the jungle. My brother RJ nearby, journeying down the same rabbit hole. The heartbeat of the forest all around.

What could be more my style than tripping on the blood of the Earth in the heart of the wild?

Something shifts. A barrier breaks.

And so it is decided: I'm in.

✦ ✦ ✦

RJ had emailed me an *ayahuasca* prep guide from a Peruvian temple he'd stayed at a while back. I read through it, but on the morning of our ceremony, I'd be lying if I said I wasn't nervous. Truthfully, I had no idea what to expect.

We roll up to Juan's around noon. I'm relieved it's happening during the day. I figure the daylight and familiar surroundings might help keep me grounded. But what I don't realize is that today will be a full-on plant medicine adventure. *Yagé*, the main course, won't arrive until evening.

My security blanket is ripped away almost immediately: Immediately upon arrival, Juan hands us a dose of *ambil* at least five times larger than our "welcome dose" and tells us to go to the river. He gives more instructions in Spanish. I watch RJ flinch slightly, then nod.

Not a good sign.

Down at the river, RJ turns to me and says, "Okay, so Juan told me we're supposed to take all of this *ambil* at once." He pauses. "It's going to make us puke."

I stare back, shaking my head. Internally, I'm all anger and expletives. What irks me more is how unaffected RJ seems now, like it's no big deal. I restrain myself as best I can, but like a fart I can't contain, I blurt out, "What the fuck?"

"Juan says if we purge now, we're less likely to later."

Alright, I can get behind that. After a moment of thinking it through, I give RJ a slight nod and sit down on a sandy patch near the river. He walks downstream and does the same.

In small doses, *ambil* tastes pungent and earthy but tolerable, almost pleasant. At this dose, it's vile. The second I try to mash it in my mouth, I gag and spit it back into my hand, flattened but still whole. It got my saliva going, though, so I let it pool. Then, I throw the mass back in, tilt my head up, and, like the oversized supplement pills I've swallowed for years, let my saliva do the work. I swallow it whole.

Instantly, the massive dose of nicotine hits my brain like a tornado, disorienting, spinning my whole world. Seconds later, I'm violently retching.

I hate this feeling. I hate this feeling.

I drop to all fours, aiming toward the clear river. The black goo, mixed with bile, pours out. I collapse onto my stomach and forearms. I stay there, eyes watering and half open, enduring the intense nausea.

I feel like such a sissy. The big, tough wrestler, down on his belly, drooling all over himself. Pathetic.

The terrible nausea lasts for what feels like forever. But then, slowly, it passes. I brace for another wave. It doesn't come.

Minutes pass. I start to feel normal again. Strong, even. I stand and go check on RJ. He doesn't look good. He tells me he took the *ambil* but didn't throw up.

We wait another twenty minutes. Still nothing. Eventually, I help RJ back to the bamboo structure. He lies down in a hammock, clearly not feeling well.

Juan meanders over and exchanges a few words with RJ. When he glances at me, I give him a sharp nod. My version of a thumbs up. They speak for another minute before Juan turns and walks away.

"What did he say?" I ask.

"He said the *ambil* was for you anyway. He's glad it worked."

"Well, what about you?"

"He says my body will release when it's ready. And that he'll check back in on us in a few hours."

"A few hours?" I echo, incredulous.

"Yeah. I'm gonna take a nap. Settle in. We'll talk soon."

After everything I just went through, it takes a while for my mind to come down. But eventually I surrender to a hammock and let the jungle's afternoon thrum carry me into a daze somewhere between sleep and stillness.

A few hours pass, and Juan is nowhere to be found. I get up and try to busy myself by taking short walks to the pond, imagining what *yagé* has in store for me. But time drags on, excruciatingly slow.

I glance over and see RJ awake in his hammock. "How you feeling?" I ask.

"Better," he says, and nothing more.

Man, I really am in Latin American standard time. What's with all the waiting? I stare at Juan's house, silently willing him to appear. He doesn't.

About half an hour later, a group of five younger men crests the ridge and walks toward us. They're dressed like transients—worn clothes, loose energy—and I don't get the best vibe from them.

I assume they're here to inquire about a future *yagé* ceremony. They exchange some words with RJ, drop their belongings, and join the wait. Another hour crawls by before Juan finally appears.

I exhale. *Here we go.*

He chats with the group for a bit, then pulls RJ aside and says something quietly. RJ returns to me a moment later.

"They're joining us," he says. "But first, Juan wants to do another ceremony in the jungle."

By now it's clear I'm not in control of any of this. And maybe that's the point. I take a breath and let go.

"Okay," I say, oddly proud of myself for managing my frustration.

A short while later, Juan appears again and motions for us to follow. A few of the guys grab their bags, but Juan quickly waves at them to leave it all behind.

We start walking, up the slope, past the great tree, and along the outer edge of a steep ravine that leads further uphill and into the jungle. It's slow going. The trail is narrow, slick, and overgrown in places. I have to watch every step as one careless move could send me sliding a long way down.

After about a half mile, we reach the end of the ravine. The terrain flattens. A waterfall spews from a crack in the rock wall, striking a wide stone on the ground before scattering into spray and recombining into a quiet stream.

Juan motions for us to sit. We spread out on both sides of the water. For a solid half hour, we sit in silence while he grinds seeds into a fine powder using a stone.

"*Yopo*," RJ whispers.

I lean toward him. "Is it psychoactive?"

He nods. "Yes, but it's short acting. About half an hour."

My nerves jolt. *Giddy up.* The moment of truth is coming. *What will I feel? What will I see?*

Once Juan is satisfied with his preparation, he stands and begins to speak. RJ translates:

"Look around you. You are safe here. This is the womb of creation. Everything here is pure. The Mother will protect you. But you must do your part. When you take the medicine, honor your mother by sitting with strength and posture. Close your eyes, and keep them closed. Do not get up and dance around like a fool. If you don't feel well, you may rest your head on your knees. Do not fall over like a baby. If you need to vomit, do so in the river, then return to a strong seated position."

RJ would later tell me that Juan was doing this ceremony as a screen to see if the younger guys had the right mindset. Whether they were ready to handle more powerful medicine. Whether they could hold themselves with respect. Whether they'd pull any "monkey business" during the *yagé* ceremony later that night.

For me, the anticipation was already enough. The intensity of it all pressed in from every side.

And then, finally, Juan was standing in front of me, loading his blowing device with powder. He motions for me to lift my chin. Then, he slides his wooden pipe just under my nostril and blasts the powder up my nose. My eyes water and I shake my head lightly. Fortunately, it doesn't burn too badly. He repeats the process in my other nostril, then moves on to RJ.

I sit up, close my eyes, slow my breath, and start coaching myself.

I've sat in meditation countless times. I'm confident in myself. Nature is my home. I know it's infused with a loving spirit. My intention is worthy. I ask for guiding light, or whatever spirit wants to show me.

Within a few minutes, I start to see a distant light forming in the darkness of my closed eyelids. I stare at it, wondering what it is, squeezing my eyes shut to try to bring it into focus.

As it starts to fill my vision, it appears to me like a fast-moving holographic band of silvery-white light. Within the light, there are figures. But I can't discern them, as they are moving from right to left so fast. As I try to make them out, I start to feel queasy.

Oh, no.

I immediately try to breathe out the feeling. It intensifies. The spinning halo of light speeds up. I start to feel my stomach turn. The nausea hits me hard, and before I know it, I'm in a squat, puking in the river.

I try to quickly compose myself, telling myself it's all better now. But then the nausea hits me again, this time even harder. Again, I'm on my knees vomiting into the river. Dry heaving now, over and over again.

And, of course, I'm the only one.

I open my eyes slightly and everything spins out of control. I catch glimpses of the others, selfishly hoping at least one other person is struggling. They look as serene as monks. It really is just me who can't handle the medicine.

Embarrassed, angry, and weak, I sit with my head on my knees. *Get me out of this hell. I don't belong here. This clearly isn't for me.*

I feel unworthy. Disappointed in myself.

I hear Juan speaking and crack my eyes open wider. The world is still spinning. The motion makes it worse. I shut them again.

Breathe. Wait. Then try once more. A little better. I see Juan standing next to the waterfall in his underwear. White, of course.

RJ leans over. "You okay?"

"I guess," I say, probably sounding like a teenager with a bad attitude.

"Juan says he wants us to come to the waterfall, one at a time, and kneel under it. He says we're supposed to release anything that's holding us back."

I watch as one of the guys strips down to his underwear and approaches the water. He's shivering and clearly afraid. Juan gestures for him to step in. He hesitates. Seconds pass, and he can't bring himself to do it. Juan walks over, puts his hand on his back, and firmly guides him forward.

He kneels. Water rushes over him. After a few seconds, he starts to leave, but Juan stops him and guides him back in. A full minute passes before Juan calls him to come out. Though I'm ashamed to admit it, even to myself, his struggle makes me feel a little better.

RJ goes next. Then Juan calls me up.

I'm so dizzy, I nearly fall over on my way to the waterfall. But I don't hesitate. The water is shockingly cold, but in my state, it's sobering. It cuts through the fog. Clears the static. I kneel. I breathe. And I ask myself what I need to let go of.

My wrestling career. My former marriage. Half a dozen other things rise and fall through my mind. I picture them all being swept down the stream, then the river, and finally to the sea, where they can be cleansed by the salt. I ask the water to wash away anything else, especially whatever lies under the surface that I can't yet name.

Juan calls to me. I rise. For the moment, I feel lighter. I wouldn't call it a baptism. But it helped. It steadied something.

After everyone has a turn under the waterfall, we make our way back along the trail toward the bamboo structure. The walk is a struggle. My legs feel heavy and off-balance. But as we near the great tree, we're bathed in sunlight.

Warming. Drying. Cleansing, in its own way.

Back at the structure, I slump down in a corner. RJ sits beside me. "Anything come up that you want to talk about?" he offers. "No pressure. But I'm here if you need it."

"I'm just… really disappointed, man," I admit. "I mean, how many times do I need to puke? And we haven't even gotten to the *yagé* yet, which is notorious for purging."

"I hear you. And yeah, man, *yagé* is unpredictable. Could be all love and light. Could be a total puke fest. Or something in between."

"Well… it's pretty obvious the plant medicines are rejecting me." I hesitate, then say it anyway: "I might opt out. I might be done."

Even saying the words makes me feel like a quitter.

RJ nods. "Think about it. We probably have at least a couple hours before the light fades and the ceremony begins. You don't have to do anything you don't want to. I totally get it."

I nod back, slouching deeper against my pack. RJ sets up for a nap nearby.

For the next hour, my mind is a battlefield. *Do I push through? Or do I take the hint and cut my losses? I don't want any more nausea. Any more shame. Maybe the timing just isn't right. Maybe I'm forcing it.*

I start packing my things. I've made the decision to bow out quietly, return to the house, and surrender to a peaceful night in bed. Then I'll continue my quest as planned, sans plant medicine.

Just as I finish zipping up my bag, Juan arrives. He looks at me, sits down on a boulder near the fire, adds a few pieces of wood to the coals, and pulls a small vial of brown powder from his bag. He speaks softly. RJ translates:

"We'll work with *rapé*. It will prepare us for what's next."

RJ explains it's made from tobacco and is taken through the nose.

"Is it going to make me throw up?" I ask, half-joking, half-fearful.

He laughs. "No, not likely."

Juan prepares the medicine and, as with the *yopo*, he blows it into each nostril, one at a time.

It burns much more than the *yopo*. Tears stream down my cheeks. But once the initial sting subsides, something shifts.

A current of energy rises up my spine. I instinctively sit upright, spine tall, legs crossed. The sensation spreads—electric, focused.

Then it reaches my mind. My thoughts change shape: *I am strong. I am healthy. I am capable. I can face whatever comes. I believe in myself. I believe in nature.*

It feels like a miracle. Like powdered courage is sparkling

in my brain. A final thought echoes through me, not loud but undeniable:

I am here for a reason. And I will see this experience through to its end.

I open my eyes. They're misty, not from the burn, but from the return of something I hadn't realized I'd lost: my power.

Juan catches the shift and gives me a half-smile along with a nod. It's the first time I've seen him break his stoic character.

I feel myself again. Not perfect, but more whole. I reclaim my inner warrior—the part of me who remembers that challenge is the fertile ground of growth. And sometimes I have to be beaten down before I can rise again, stronger and better.

Night sweeps in, transforming the vibrant valley into a sea of shadow and starlight. We all gather near the fire pit, taking turns feeding it. The flames twist and spiral upward, forming a beacon of light in the darkening landscape.

Juan approaches and settles onto his boulder. I notice an old liter soda bottle filled with a thick, brown liquid in tow.

The main event has arrived.

I'm nervous, but no longer consumed by fear. I'm ready, optimistic, but not naive.

After an opening invocation, the first cup arrives. The brew tastes earthy and sharp.

I sit tall. Breathe deep. RJ had told me it's best to lie down with *yagé*, so I ease back onto my towel and stare at the ceiling, waiting.

A few minutes pass. Then I start to hear music. Latin American-sounding, but with an odd, circus-like edge. It unsettles me. I start to pray:

Dear God, please have mercy on me. I seek truth, but I beg you, no more suffering. Please protect me. Please teach me in the gentlest way possible.

The music fades. A strange sensation begins building in my neck, a familiar place of tension—years of wrestling and weightlifting have made it nearly permanent. But this is different. It tightens more and more, until my neck arches completely off the ground.

Then a voice: clear, loud, unmistakably my own:

"Danny, welcome to the dojo of life."

What the…?

"I'm going to teach you a few things today. And since you asked for mercy, you'll receive it."

Thank you. Thank you. Thank you…

"Now I've given you a riddle. Your neck tension. Solve it."

Okay, I reply inwardly.

I run through everything I've learned over the years. I try light stretching. Nothing. I slow my breathing. Hold it. Exhale with intention. Still stiff. As a last-ditch effort, I try *talking* to my neck. *Relax. Please relax.*

No change.

Finally, I give up. *What can I do?* I ask.

At that exact moment, I feel a tap on my shoulder. I open my eyes and see RJ, propped on one elbow.

"This might help," he says, handing me my phone and headphones.

I slip them on. Unlock the screen. My hands move as if not fully my own. I type in the search function of my music app: "Spirit Horses," an instrumental by Brulé, a Native American band. My dad used to play the song on fishing trips. I press play.

The opening melody hits me. A soft chant… then a dreamy, pulsing beat.

Tears fill my eyes. Like magic, my neck tension *melts.*

And then the main beat arrives, an entourage of flute and rhythm. My back arches, lifting my chest to the sky. I feel my space around my heart expand in a way I've never felt before.

I feel strange but familiar, like I'm a child again. Like innocence is pouring back into me. Then the voice returns, radiant with intensity:

"This is love, Danny. Love is all that is pure. All that is true. All that is inspiring. It is the only antidote. The only solution. The only true way. It is the pride of my creation. The truth of nature. The force that is me…"

I can't respond, too caught in the moment. The power of this experience is the highest high I've ever felt. I feel like I'm riding a wave in outer space.

"What you call life, Danny, I call love. And I'm going to give you a drill to remember it. Love was—and is—created through my breath. Take a deep breath in."

I inhale.

The song reaches its climax and the melody breaks open into a flood of layered, triumphant sound.

"Now, let it go."

I exhale.

And then, a vision. The most vivid, powerful imagery I've ever seen: Stars igniting. Galaxies forming. Oceans swirling into vortices. DNA weaves itself from crystallized light.

Beings of all kinds—fish, dinosaurs, rabbits, birds—morphing into one another, striving to further life. Then, humans. Walking across vast deserts, holding the hands of their children. Afraid, but guided by the love burning in their hearts.

"Heart first, Danny. When you lead with your heart, you lead with me. And I will always protect you."

Is that why I was throwing up so much? Because I was leading with my head?

"Bingo. You have a strong mind, Danny. But you're not that smart. I am the ultimate intelligence. And I've given you a much greater gift: your heart. I want you to listen with it and use it. Do you understand?"

Yes.

And with that one word, reinforced by the feeling in my chest, I finally do.

"Good. Now, next lesson."

My eyes are closed. In the blackness, I see the same holographic halo I saw with the *yopo*. But this time, I'm not nauseous. I'm not afraid. My heart is open. I feel protected. The halo is no longer spinning at a distance. It's flowing *into* me.

I begin to see intricate geometric patterns, mostly triangles and star shapes. They shift and transform, turning brilliant colors. A few of them hover and dance as if welcoming me... celebrating my return to somewhere I've been before.

A dream? I wonder.

Then, I see myself sitting by a river in the jungle.

I'm still aware of my body lying on the ground in the bamboo structure, so I don't feel fear. If I open my eyes, I can still see the space around me, though everything is faintly overlaid with a holographic shimmer.

But when I close my eyes, I return to the river. I'm seated there, entranced, staring into the swirling water. No words are spoken. But I'm learning—the river is teaching me.

An understanding emerges: Evolution is more than survival. It's a gradual refinement through suffering—not in spite of suffering but *through* its pressure. Evolution is a crucible that slowly forges heart-centered awareness, which, when blended with gut-level courage, becomes a mechanism of action that is fueled by passionate, authentic drive. And when that type of drive blossoms within us, the mind becomes a servant to the heart rather than the limiting beliefs we are indoctrinated to. And thus, the creative force within us is freed. Not just to preserve life but to create beauty unlike anything the world has seen before.

I open my eyes, mind spinning as I try to grasp what I've just received. When I close them again, the scene has changed: I'm watching a creature—something between a hedgehog and an armadillo—tucked tightly into a ball, rolling through a maze.

It uncurls, stopping itself from rolling. Slowly, it rises and begins to walk. It pauses, then starts again, and I know this time it is using its heart to navigate toward the center of the labyrinth.

I understand the message instantly: *This is what it means to live with purpose.*

The real work of life is learning to lead with the heart. Not just as an emotion of longing, but as an instrument of receiving higher guidance. A bridge between self and spirit. To lead with the heart means learning to be led by the presence within and infused in the world around us. It takes courage, receptivity, and a quiet trust in something wiser than the mind. Too often, we meet the intensity of that labyrinth by curling inward, into fear, anxiety, shame, and confusion.

It's understandable: Reality *is* intense. But if we stay in that shape, we roll through life blindly until we die. When we believe in the good—in our innocence, in ourselves, in the intelligence of nature, in the possibility of a brighter future—we uncurl. And in that uncurling, we begin to hear the guidance that was always there, from a presence beyond the mind, conveying a truth far greater than life and death.

The scene fades. I open my eyes. Then I hear the voice again: "Write it down."

I open the Notes app and type a few cryptic lines, just enough to anchor what I've seen and learned. Then I set the phone down, close my eyes, and let my body relax, trying to process it all.

The voice returns: "Any questions?"

I think: *I want to understand the connection between nature and spirit.*

"I have told you. Now I'll show you."

The halo of light hovers before me. It contracts into a ball, slowly spinning. It starts to look like a planet, but not solid. It looks like it's made of some kind of goo, like those sticky green balls I played with as a child.

The goo shifts color—shimmering greens, blues, golds—then begins to form shapes. Not geometric this time. Familiar things: a tree, a rock, a monkey.

All made of goo. All emerging from and returning to the same substance.

Then the ball drifts closer, right in front of my face. The surface shifts like an art exhibit. First patterns, like those I've seen on Navajo rugs. Then Monet. Then Picasso. Then blood red tiles, like a strange floor, each with a human arm sticking out.

No words. No explanation. Only clear insight: *This is the life force. It's everything.*

The vision dissolves. And the voice whispers one last time:

"I'm always here, Danny. I'm always here."

I sit up.

Others are gathered around the fire now, so I join them. In the firelight, I notice a line of ants moving along the bamboo structure, resolute in their purpose. A deep gratitude rises within me. I offer them a quiet bow, honoring their life force and their role in the great, evolving story of life.

Later that night, Juan leads the closing ceremony. He speaks a few words, then spits herbal liquor over us. Before we leave, I walk up to him.

He gives that same quiet half-smile and gently beats his fist against his chest. *"Corazón,"* he says firmly, proudly.

"Corazón," I echo, fist on heart.

IV: TREASURE

After the ceremony, I don't come back glowing. I come back quiet. Something inside of me had cracked open, and now it needs to take root. I won't read as much as I was before; I need to let my experiences integrate and digest in stillness.

The jungle gave me a huge dose of clarity, but Vermont is the test: Can I carry what I've seen and felt into the grind of daily life?

I return to Vermont with a more practical mindset: I'll refurbish the toolshed and make it habitable, so I can take my time with the stone cabin project without constant pressure to finish. Though I still call the smaller structure the "toolshed," it was originally built as a 400-square-foot house with a spacious loft. With a few upgrades and additions, it'll make a fine temporary tiny home.

The initial stages are cold and lonely. But I've saved enough to hire a local carpenter, and together we chip away at the work. By the time the weather warms, I'm lounging under the covered porch, cooking outside, and feeling the quiet pleasure of progress. Soon I'll have power. Running water. Luxuries I haven't had in over a year.

As my living situation stabilizes, I notice something else beginning to bloom. A curiosity. A quiet ache. I start to open up to a deeper relationship with a woman. Not just companionship; I enjoy being alone. Honestly, I can't quite put my finger on the feeling. It's not logical. Not urgent. Just… present.

I remove "not looking for anything serious" from my online dating profile. *What can it hurt?*

Within a few days, I check my phone and discover that I have messages from three different women, all named Megan. One spells it with an H, Meghan.

Odd, I think. It's been three years since my divorce, and I've never even been on a date with anyone with that name. Now suddenly, I've matched with three.

Each of them seems to hold a different energy: One is clearly into fitness—bright spandex, barbells, Barbie-esque bleached-blonde hair.

Another has the look of a seductress—dark features and alluring eyes that seem to say, *Come and get me.*

The third—the Meghan with an H—lands somewhere in the middle. Round cheeks, bright blue eyes, a jovial smile. Her photos hint at adventure.

Deep down, I know this is a test. Will I go for the fitness look, a reflection of my past? The seductress, a mirror of my present hunger? Or will I choose the adventure girl, a reflection of my deeper self, what I'm slowly reclaiming?

Something about Meghan speaks to an ancient feeling. A recognition of sorts. And an interest that feels… timeless. Far deeper than the physical. And, interestingly enough, she's the first one willing to set up a date, a walk in the woods by her house.

It's a beautiful day in early May, and spring is in full force. The dense Vermont forest is smiling with thousands of vibrant green buds. The soil smells warm and musky, radiating life. It feels as if nature woke up overnight and burst into action.

I drive over the mountains to another quaint little town. Butterflies dance in both the fields and in my stomach as I take the final turn toward her house. I roll into the driveway and see her standing outside, cheeks pulled back in a bright, welcoming smile.

The moment I see her, a wave of relaxation washes over me, as if I'm meeting a dear friend for the first time. Her presence doesn't evoke eroticism. It touches something more pure. Innocent. Joyful.

"Hi, I'm Meghan," she says as we share a quick hug.

I introduce myself, and without much small talk, we set off into the woods. She leads me up a steep hill, and I'm already impressed with her endurance. Nothing in her profile mentioned fitness. She's dressed modestly in a loose turquoise shirt and black capris. As I huff and puff, I prod a bit into her background and learn she ran track in college. *She's soft, yet tough*, I think to myself, my excitement growing quietly within.

We reach the top of a long ridgeline overlooking a stunning valley. The scene looks geometric in its bold, overlapping hills, yet picturesque in its blend of soft colors, like a classic Vermont painting by Sabra Field.

While we sit for a bit, she tells me she's a teacher at an elementary school in Boston. She studied philosophy and writing, and she's passionate about helping kids develop the skills they need to thrive. I tell her that I teach movement, with a similar passion for helping people feel strong and capable so they can live more powerful lives.

She says she has a few lingering injuries, so I show her a couple of movements that might help. We both catch a case of the giggles, then continue our walk.

We end up on a dirt road leading to an old town hall. In front of the building, a statue catches our attention—a mountain lion, fierce and splendid, frozen in a stalking position, muscles rippling beneath its skin.

We sit by a nearby tree and talk for a while. Everything feels so perfect, but I feel the need to be honest. I tell her I have a child. That I've been married. That I live in a shack, off-grid. Philosophically, I don't believe in love as ownership. I ramble, spitting out all my baggage, in a way testing her ability to handle me. Secretly, I'm hoping I won't scare her off, but I'm also fully expecting that I might.

"Oh, I don't know about all that," she says. "But I think I just want to kiss you."

I slowly lift my gaze from her mouth to her azure-colored eyes. Our lips touch, and a lightness comes over me that, until now, I've only felt in solitude, embraced by nature. It's pure magic, and I surrender to the purity of the moment.

As we walk back, she shows me a piece of quartz she found nearby, crystal clear and textured with a hint of smoke. What a lucky find, I think. She tells me that since she's come home from Boston and returned to nature, she feels like she's reclaiming her true self. I give a quiet nod, reflecting on how I feel the same way.

We stroll together effortlessly, and I say something along the lines of: "You know, according to quantum physics, there is no physical matter, just attraction and repulsion. So we're not actually making contact with the ground when we walk. We're being repelled by it."

Inwardly, I think, *I'm such a dork. I probably just blew the whole moment.*

She takes my hands and says, "That's exactly how I feel right now. Like I'm floating."

I look up at the trees crowning overhead, stunned by her presence, how effortlessly she meets me where I am. Not just in intellect but in spirit. There's no posturing, no pretending. Just this mutual openness, this natural wonder humming between us like a secret song we both know.

Back at her place, we say goodbye with another brief kiss. Nothing dramatic. Just enough to seal the magic of the day. As I drive away, I glance in the rearview mirror and feel something timeless settle quietly in my chest, like a stone placed carefully in the foundation of a future I didn't even know I was building.

This time, I'm not chasing the feeling. I'm walking with it.

During the next few weeks, we live in a kind of cloud, suspended in the ethereal bliss of what can only be called love. It catches me by surprise, but I don't resist. I let it move through me. The feeling is too sweet and dreamy in the merging of mind and body, yet somehow grounded in the fertile mountain forests of Vermont.

Meghan moves in, and we begin building a new dream together. It's a softer one with fewer aggressive timelines and far less hard labor. A vision that still includes a home but also more walks along ancient riverbeds, more meandering upon trails padded with pine needles and golden leaf litter.

We both push each other to grow in new ways. She introduces me to the wonder of crystals, adding words like *labradorite* and *rose quartz* to my vocabulary. She also shares *The Alchemist* with me, a book that opens my mind to the more feminine idea of omens, signs from the "soul of the world" that guide us through life.

I help her grow more comfortable living close to the earth, holding snakes for the first time, and bathing in the cold, clear river. I guide her back to her physical body, helping her reclaim her athleticism in a more balanced, nature-centered way.

We spend the rest of the summer working on the small cabin together, slowly making it feel like a real home. And even though no progress is being made on the big stone cabin, Sacred Acres feels more complete than ever.

Meghan and my son develop a special bond, sharing a quiet resonance for finding things in nature—rocks, feathers, newts, and countless other treasures. They call it *treasure hunting*. Searching for sacred pieces of the land becomes part of our daily rhythm when he's with us.

One day, while walking near the homesite, Meg finds *the blue guy*—the little Lego man my son had lost the year before. I take it as an omen, a clear sign of her ability to help us both find the parts of ourselves we thought were gone.

Everything feels perfect and whole. I feel like nature is taking care of me. And for the first time, I experience a genuine acceptance of Vermont, even though it's nothing like the wild Rocky Mountain dream I once clung to.

And then, as if on cue, it all begins to fall apart.

First, COVID-19 hits. My event-based education business takes a major blow. The world shifts to remote learning, and I'm under pressure to film more e-courses to meet the demand. But producing them in the rural, often harsh conditions of Vermont becomes increasingly difficult.

Then comes the huge blow. What had already been a disharmonious co-parenting relationship with my ex-wife, Amy, escalates into an outright rupture. She withholds my visitation rights, saying I can only see my son if I rent a hotel, citing my outhouse as the rationale.

This isn't just a disagreement—it's the tip of an iceberg that I've been trying to manage for years. I'm fuming. Ready to fight. But beneath the anger, a quieter voice begins to rise. It urges me not to fight her. Instead, visions come. Glimpses of the rocky high desert of New Mexico. Sunlight, stone, and sky flood my mind. I feel a longing for open space. For warmth. For clarity. A line I first heard years ago echoes through me like a mantra:

Where the desert meets the mountains. That's where I belong.

Even my soundtrack shifts. The soft, tranquil beats I usually play in the car are replaced by the low, rebellious thunder of *Wherever I May Roam*. I think of my road trip. My youth. That raw fire is returning. It's as if the soul of the world is throwing omens now into my mindspace, guiding me back toward the Rocky Mountain dream I never fully released.

Then, one sunny summer day, comes the final straw. A

representative from the state of Vermont shows up at the cabin—prompted, I later learn, by a complaint questioning the legality of my water system. I can't read him at first. He's a rugged, well-kept older gentleman.

Maybe he's a by-the-book enforcer who will nail me for using a spring with a simple drainage system for my greywater until my property's septic system is installed. Or maybe he's a good-ol'-boy Vermonter who'll understand my situation, given that I'm in the middle of a permitted build. If it's the former, I'm in trouble.

"I'm here from the state of Vermont to take a look at your water situation," he says, matter-of-fact.

"Yes, sir," I reply, offering to show him around.

He walks the land slowly—studying the stone construction in the distance, the uninstalled septic tank, my building permit, the small cabin, and eventually, the spring. Finally, he turns to me. For a moment, he gives me nothing. Then a faint smile curls at the corner of his mouth.

"So why am I really here?" he asks.

"That's a good question," I say. "Honestly, I think my ex-wife is determined to make my life difficult."

He laughs lightly, shaking his head. "I can see that. I don't see any problems here. At the very least, you don't have to worry about the state of Vermont. The rest… well. I wish you luck."

That night, I tell Meghan what happened. She's shaken. Like me, she's worn down by the relentlessness of it all. We sit together in the weight of the realization: This isn't just about my relationship with my son anymore. It's about our home. Our stability. Our well-being.

Then Meg asks, gently, "What's in your heart?"

She pauses. "I've heard you talk about living out west before. Are you sure you even belong here?"

I sit with her words. I tell her I've always felt called to the

West. That I've been having visions of New Mexico. I say it with shame, as if confessing a betrayal—like even thinking it makes me a bad father.

"I think you're a fantastic father," she says. "But you can't be the father you're meant to be under this kind of pressure. It's not fair to you. And it's not fair to your son."

Her words land hard.

I think about my son—how he's been showing signs of anxiety, and his ears keep mysteriously burning and turning red. Maybe it's the things he hears. Maybe it's the strain of moving between two very different households. Either way, I can feel it in him. He's carrying the tension, too.

She's right. This isn't fair to him.

It also becomes clear that my presence isn't helping Amy, either. In my idealism, I thought staying close was the right thing to do. But instead of easing the transition, it's only prolonging the friction—for both of us.

Then I consider my work: My role with the educational company based in New Mexico. The access to filming resources. The support system is already in place.

I try to remove my own dreams from the equation. But no matter how I approach it, the answer is the same: It's time to make a change. It's time to go where the desert meets the mountains.

My son takes the news better than I expect. With Meghan's help, we walk him through everything—maps, pictures, timelines. When we talk about fishing out west, his face lights up.

I sell the property to a young couple eager to leave the city and carry the permaculture vision forward in their own way. The transition unfolds with surprising ease. But for me, the move is gut-wrenching. Amy resists every step. At times, the stress manifests as a literal, searing pain in my stomach as my body processes what my mind is trying to endure.

Through it all, Meg stays beside me—steady, protective, unwavering.

She shows me that love can be more than feelings. For us, it's also structure. Like the Vermont bedrock beneath the forests where we met, our love steadies us to bear the weight of what we are building together.

And so we pack.

On my thirty-sixth birthday, we drive up the steep grade of the Rockies and roll into New Mexico beneath a wide turquoise sky.

AIR

1: ARRIVAL

THIS TIME, I'M determined to make it work in the Rockies.

After being kicked out so many times, I'm uneasy. I don't want to be forced back east for any reason. I can't endure the heartbreak of seeing my dream crushed again.

But as we drive up the steep grade of the Colorado Plateau, it no longer feels like a pursuit. It feels like an awakening. I understand now that for the mountains to truly receive me, the rest of my life must be in alignment.

For the first time, I'm not arriving empty-handed or full of hot air. A stable job is anchoring me out west. A woman who shares my vision of living beyond the clockwork of society and attuning to the older rhythms of the earth walks beside me. And I carry with me a deeper clarity regarding the burning questions that have always drawn me to these mountains.

But I've come to realize something else: It's not just the answers that move me forward. It's the willingness to keep asking deeper, more disruptive questions—the kind that stretch me beyond stability, reveal truths larger than I imagined, and inspire me into meaningful motion. The ones that offer no promise of comfort, only honesty.

And somewhere along the way, I've stopped waiting for permission to ask them. I've learned to trust that if a question continues to rise, again and again, it's because it's meant to be asked. And, most importantly, I have the ability to receive and understand the answers, as they come to me.

And now I'm heading to a place where I feel ready to ask the most profound questions. The kind that could split the sky open and teach me how to fly.

One question in particular rises to the surface: *What unseen current connects the voice I've heard, the visions I've seen, and the creative force of love moving through nature?*

I don't know the answer yet, but I can feel it, close. Like heat shimmering above a trail just ahead.

I've followed this pull to nature for years—trusting instinct, chasing dreams, letting the land guide me without always knowing why. And step by step, the deeper pattern has begun to reveal itself. Now, in the clarity of high desert air, my awareness sharpens. And, further, I see myself more clearly:

I am a tracker. Not of reptiles and amphibians anymore, as in my youth.

Of truth.

And its ancient scent hangs pungent in the wind of this fiery landscape, pulling me forward with its magnetic allure.

These insights and countless others ripple through me as we snake around 14,000-foot peaks, descend into the vast alpine cradle of the San Luis Valley, and cross into northern New Mexico.

I think of Hermes—messenger of the gods, guide of travelers, guardian of thresholds—and wonder what this next chapter will teach me. Whatever is waiting to unfold in this sage-ridden sea of potential, one thing is crystal clear: within moments of arriving in New Mexico, it already has me enchanted in its primordial spell.

I feel why so many seekers are drawn to this land. Something timeless lingers in the air, speaking through these mountains.

Something alive.

We arrive at our place, a small garage converted into a guesthouse. Our landlords, a couple in their eighties, are warm and full of quiet grace. The front of our little home is nearly all windows, facing east toward the grandeur of the Sangre de Cristo Mountains.

Translated as "Blood of Christ," these peaks glow brilliant red each evening at sunset. They radiate a heavenly presence, like a shimmering veil between us and whatever still lingers from the life we left behind. Guardians, in their own way. Silent, luminous, and watching.

We get right to work, not just filming courses for the business I run, but on deepening our connection to this new place. Meghan and I visit a local healer who helps release what she describes as "energetic cords," i.e., residual ties to the past that siphon energy and vitality. She scans our bodies using her mind's eye, looking for places of tension or some other signal she's trained to recognize. She finds a cord in my solar plexus the size of a tree trunk. She puts her feet on my hips and rips it out while I visualize it being removed.

I struggle to comprehend what it all means. Logically, it makes no sense. But I can't deny what follows: Once removed, I feel a gaping hollowness where the cord once was. The acidic burn and tension I've carried in that spot for months immediately begin to ease. Within days, the pain lifts completely. Something lets go. And whether or not my mind can explain it, my body knows it's real.

Another form of inner work is also beginning to blossom. All my seeking has finally shaped itself into a unique path. What began in Vermont as reading and experimentation has slowly matured into an understanding. And a practice. I'm no longer chasing truth so much through philosophies, books, and frameworks. Instead, I'm learning to trust that nature is my teacher. And to receive its lessons, I have to enter its classroom—outside, on the Earth, in the sunlight and air.

✦ ✦ ✦

In Vermont, I developed certain techniques to enter a trance-like state. I'd gaze into nature, quieting my mind's compulsion to name, sort, and analyze. When I fixed my attention on a single point, something would eventually shift. My perception would soften and widen. Shapes began to shimmer. Colors and movements emerged. Not random, but patterned. Communicative.

In those moments, much like during my *yagé* visions, I began to receive teachings. Not in words, but in form and feeling. Insights would eventually flow through me like a waterfall: echoes of timeless truths conveyed through the fabric of creation. Nature was showing me things. About life and about myself.

This deepened through a budding relationship with traditional plant medicines. *Yagé* had already been powerful, but now another substance of the Earth began calling to me.

At a friend's bachelor party in Vermont, I'd taken my first dose of magic mushrooms. The experience was a revelation. I felt more alive, more focused, more attuned. My senses sharpened. My sight expanded. Shimmering geometric shapes danced in the air—patterns pulsing with meaning.

Then came the insight, clear and unmistakable:

Mushrooms will help me pierce the veil and see into the governing forces of nature. They can help me navigate my path.

It became no mystery why some call them "magic," or even, in certain esoteric circles, the "philosopher's stone."

When I combined mushrooms with my trance work, true magic began to unfold. The veil between me and nature thinned. I could see more clearly through the solidity of form and into the flowing lattice of the land.

They also helped me see more clearly into my own mind and taught me to trust my inner vision. With their help, my capacity to learn soared like an eagle, offering a new, elevated perspective shaped by rich experiences in nature.

In Vermont, I had become open to the idea of omens. In New Mexico, that openness deepened into something more. Omens were no longer fragmentary signals that I half-believed, such as seeing 11:11 on my phone. Built on the scaffolding of what fire, water, and earth had each taught me, I could now recognize them as a real language from the world, ushered through nature. They came as visual communications and lessons that spoke not just to my intuition, but to my logical mind as well. They became something I trusted fully, an ongoing conversation with nature.

Any time a question arose, a response would follow, often within minutes or hours. Sometimes it came as a spontaneous vision in my mind's eye.

For example, one afternoon I wanted to understand how planets are formed. I asked the question during a short meditation outdoors and forgot about it shortly after. Later, I felt a quiet pull, a subtle nudge to close my eyes and look inward. And there it was: vortices of light, spinning and condensing as if shaped by invisible hands. Even if I couldn't fully grasp the physics, the vision gave me a more intuitive visual understanding of energy, rotation, consolidation, and expansion. I could see the elemental forces of nature collaborating in the act of creation.

It felt like having a personal science teacher within, fluent in the language of nature and capable of unlocking the mysteries behind anything that stirred my curiosity, including more everyday societal issues.

Other times, it arrived through the outer world: a heart-shaped rock in my path. A card drawn from an oracle deck. A strange synchronicity. A better ability to see the difference between modern marketing and more timeless communications. All experiences that led to insights that inspired the right kind of action in my daily life.

✦ ✦ ✦

And yet, even in the midst of these illuminations, as we settle in New Mexico, the practicalities of daily life loop through my mind. A key question:

Where will we find our home?

I ask this question each day, spending hours scouting listings on Zillow. We've saved enough for a down payment from the sale of the Vermont property, and I'm determined to find a place of our own. We've learned that we don't want to build a house from scratch again. Other work calls us now, and we don't want to become overburdened or trapped in another unstable situation.

What we want is a home base. A place we can expand upon, root into, and grow from.

About two months after we arrived in New Mexico, I'm sitting in the front yard among the sagebrush one afternoon when something incredible happens: Three rainbows appear over the mountains. One directly in front of me and a double rainbow off to the south.

A wave of déjà vu washes over me. I've seen this before, whether in a dream or some liminal space I once passed through, I can't say. I rise to my feet, scanning the sky, and suddenly I see rainbows everywhere. Arching shapes shimmer faintly in the air, like echoes.

I trace them with my eyes, following the lines of light. When I reach the end of the double rainbow, I hear it clearly:

Here is where you'll find your treasure.

I run inside to tell Meghan, pointing urgently toward the mesas and mountains to the south. "That's where we'll find our house," I tell her.

"Okay," she replies, not fully comprehending but accepting my words.

I narrow my search to that area, remembering a house I saw in that exact direction. In fact, it was the very first listing I came across when I started looking back in Vermont. I'd saved it even though it was far beyond our budget.

But now, after what I just experienced, I feel compelled to book a showing. *Why not?* I've always believed I'd find some kind of miracle deal on a house others overlooked simply because it was too far from society.

Could this be it?

We meet the real estate agent on a narrow bridge over a large flowing river, just before an old train station that looks like it belongs to another time. From there, we follow her for miles up a bumpy, winding dirt road that steadily climbs up the side of the gorge. In several spots, it winds dangerously close to shear drop-offs.

I glance at Meghan, concerned that the road might be making her anxious. "You okay?" I ask.

"Yes," she replies, nodding. I can tell she's a little shaken, but her demeanor is calm and steady.

We finally arrive. The view is stunning, overlooking a mighty gorge carved by an ancient river. Across the river, textured foothills lead up toward the bulging spine of the Rockies in the distance.

And the house is more than I imagined. The moment I step inside, I'm flooded with emotion. It's the same style and blueprint as the stone cabin I had started to build in Vermont: a simple rectangular earthen base with a timber-framed top. Completely off-grid.

I step outside and spot an undeniable omen: the same red Honda generator I once cherished in Vermont, now staring back at me like an old friend.

To top it off, the house sits cradled in a legion of rocky formations near the top of the mesa. Behind it lies nothing but wild, undeveloped land. Untamed, open, and free.

When Meghan and I talk, she says, "I feel like this is it."

I nod. "I do too." I turn to the agent. "How many people have made offers on this house?"

"None," she says. "The few who braved the road didn't want to deal with it." She shrugs, amused.

"Well, we don't have a problem with it," I tell her.

She smiles, something knowing in her eyes. "I feel like this place is meant to be yours."

A few days later, we make the highest offer we can, which is hundreds of thousands below the asking price. The seller accepts. It's a deal.

Somewhere beyond the ridge, the land exhales, welcoming us home.

11: DRIFT

We move into our new house in December. It's cold, and we have to adjust quickly, lighting fires, learning the off-grid electrical system, and tuning into the rhythms of the land. But the bright sun is a welcome reprieve after the long gray of Vermont winters.

And we're ecstatic. For the first time, we're in a stable place of our own, nested in a landscape where we truly belong.

The house is perfect for us. Huge picture windows frame the view. Light and jade plants fill the south-facing sunroom. Raw tree-trunk-lined stairs lead to a spacious loft that we convert to a bedroom on one side, a zen-like movement space on the other. For the first time in years, we can exhale. We settle into the rhythm of our new life.

It's not long before we begin venturing into the wilderness behind our home. The black basalt is a remnant of ancient volcanic force, echoing the land's timeless power. A wide sandy wash winds toward white, weathered sandstone formations. Hauntingly beautiful, they jut toward the sky like natural cathedrals. In the other direction, a treed canyon drops to the river, a cool, heavy contrast balancing the mesa's airy light.

We make a habit of wandering, searching for treasures. Meghan finds arrowheads made of obsidian. On one warm spring day, she discovers a large quartzite point in a wash near the river.

I start making solo ventures a weekly routine, exploring further into the unknown. In my mind, I begin mapping the terrain. I give names to the formations, e.g., Gem Mountain and St. John's Tower.

Then something strange begins to happen: When I return to certain places, names I've never heard before start rising into my consciousness. While climbing one lava formation I feel particularly drawn to, a word keeps surfacing:

Yebbitz

It repeats like a whisper. Eventually, I look it up. In Hebrew, it means "the rocks." Since the word came to me while on rocks, I don't discount it. Rather, I accept *Yebbitz* as the name of that particular rock formation.

Then another name begins to rise from nowhere in particular, just floating into my awareness:

Yukenstasal

That one doesn't translate to anything, but somehow, I know what it means. It feels like the name of the land itself, the whole area. As if the land is speaking to me, introducing itself.

Meghan continues to find treasures. Her favorite is a mineral called staurolite, which is shaped like a crooked cross and studded with tiny garnets. When she looks it up, she finds the common name: *fairy crosses*. Sometimes she discovers perfect 90-degree ones, like miniature sacred artifacts. They feel special, charged with meaning. She begins making small altars around the house, arranging her finds with care. Then she starts noticing the hardened amber clumps of resin scattered near dead piñon trees and begins burning them on charcoal discs, filling the house with their rich and grounding scent.

We begin to realize we can shift the energy of the home—and thus, ourselves—simply by burning what the trees offer. It makes the house feel more like an extension of the land. Like it's alive.

On my solo journeys, I begin weaving in a practice I first explored in Vermont: wearing headphones and letting music guide me. I choose tracks that match the mood of the land—cedar flutes, gentle guitars, soft, introspective electronic beats. The music gives voice to the terrain and shapes my movement. It offers a rhythm to the pace of my steps, syncing with the sway of cacti and clouds. It turns the mesa into a moving myth.

I begin to see these outings less as walks and more as quests for deeper lessons about nature and life. I start referring to them as my "wisdom quests." The land becomes a living classroom, filled with obstacles, omens, and dynamic teachings. It presents me with a clear step forward in following my calling. A quantum leap in learning, far beyond anything I experienced in Vermont.

I learn to vary my pace and to use plant medicines like mush-rooms and *rapé*, the tobacco I was introduced to in Colombia, to move between active and receptive phases. Sometimes I hike hard, feeling the fire in my lungs. Other times I sit still, listening. Movement gives way to meditation; effort yields to observation.

Each phase reveals something different. Together, they form an exercise of deeper learning.

A new kind of fitness, one that forges both body and mind through natural rhythm rather than reps.

Deep insights push through in unexpected moments. I

notice that when I'm thinking about my life, my ego-mind is still present, strategizing how to infuse spirituality into my work, planning immersive experiences. But when I just move and listen without worrying about my place in the world, something more profound begins to rise. Philosophical insights bubble through, unforced.

Simple. Expansive. Alive.

I am God, experiencing my own mind.

I am nature, experiencing itself.

And I begin to find treasures of my own. A piece of driftwood shaped like a snake catches my eye. Something in it shifts my focus from strength training to working on my flexibility. The snake elicits an insight:

Move through the land with not just power but fluidity.

Then come the rocks. I keep finding slabs marked with cryptic symbols—patterns etched or stained into the surface, like some ancient code that only my mushroom-sharpened vision can detect. I begin seeing the same motif in clouds, in tree bark, even in the visions that emerge during deep meditation. It begins to feel familiar, ubiquitous—as if a single pattern is wearing many forms.

My trance work deepens. I slip more easily into states of merging with the land, where perception blurs and boundaries dissolve. One color begins appearing again and again: magenta. It pulses in my inner vision, guiding my gaze, carrying messages too deep to name. I don't try to translate them. I just let them move through me. Gradually, the pattern I've been seeing begins to feel less like coincidence and more like a current. And it fills me with an unshakable joy to be alive and tracking it.

I continue to read, but now with a sense of detachment. I see truth in everything, yet nothing quite touches the mark of what I'm actually doing.

The closest echo appears in the most esoteric passages of Patanjali's *Yoga Sutras*. He describes a refined state of meditation called *samyama*—where the distinction between observer and observed dissolves, where inner and outer collapse into one. He writes that from this state arise *siddhis*—unusual capacities that most would call magical.

Interesting. But what could magic possibly have to do with nature?

Nature is practical, stable, and enduring. Enchanted, yes, but not magical. Nature is real. Magic is not.

Like most people, I've long assumed magic belongs to fakery and fairy tales of sorcerers and tricksters trying to control nature for selfish gain. Even if magic were real, I'd still consider it manipulative, dangerous, egoic. Something not worth touching.

And yet…here I am, stumbling across ancient practices I've never studied. And nature itself seems to be guiding me toward something hidden at the heart of magic. The thought unsettles me enough to bring it up with Meghan. She tells me, without hesitation, that she believes in magic. She often falls asleep watching a show called *Merlin*, so I ask if I can watch it with her.

The story follows a young magician, Merlin, born with innate gifts. He's called to the mythical city of Camelot to serve the king. In this version, the king is Uther, a tyrant who has banned magic to preserve order and safety. He fears its destructive potential. But in doing so, he condemns the innocent and oppresses his own people. Merlin becomes the servant of Uther's heir, Prince Arthur, secretly using magic to protect him.

While the story is rich with symbolism and ethical complexity, two things in particular stand out. The first is Merlin's encounters with other sorcerers, where they speak of the *source* of magic, called the *old religion*. Over time, this religion is revealed to be a relationship with the forces of nature.

The second is Merlin's true quest, which isn't to hide magic but to integrate it. To help Prince Arthur unite magic and civilization under his eventual rule. To usher in a new era called *Albion*, meaning "the white land."

I mull this over for a while. I don't know what to make of it. I hope the land can offer clarity, because I'm starting to feel confused about where this is all leading. Part of me fears I'm stumbling into something dangerous. But another part—the part that's been quietly awakening—wonders:

What if this isn't just a fairytale? What if it's a prophecy? An omen, in story form. A glimpse of human evolution. But also a warning about what happens when power is severed from reverence. A prompt to turn potential into prosperity.

I don't want to become ungrounded.

I've learned that every moment of illumination must be met with an equal descent into doubt. Not to destroy the insight, but to test it, to see what remains when ego is removed. I commit to a kind of alchemical discipline: for every revelation, I question my own bias and search for the counterpoint grounded in logic and rooted in science.

For the next few months, I wrap myself in doubt out of devotion to discovering the truth. I trust it as a blade that slices through illusion and leaves only what can withstand scrutiny.

I make requests of nature: Help me become a scientist. Help me move beyond passive learning. Help me ask the real questions, the ones no textbook I've encountered dares to answer directly:

What evidence is there that magic is woven into nature itself?

Is evolution really just random mutation filtered by environment, with no deeper intelligence involved?

Why would suffering, illness, and death exist in a world described as magical?

And beneath those questions lies a deeper one: *Consciousness—what is it, really? Where does it live?*

The answers don't come as arguments. They come as images that rise in my mind without effort. As patterns that repeat while I walk the land. I don't treat them as absolutes, but rather as clues. Then I test them against what I learned from my biology degree, as well as what I can observe in nature.

I learn to hold opposing perspectives without rushing to resolve them. Instead of forcing a verdict, I let the tension remain. I let paradox do its work. And slowly, something clearer begins to form. Not compromise. Integration. A way of seeing that honors both reason and reverence.

Over months of wrestling with doubt, four simple understandings take shape:

1. Magic is already present in nature.

The fact that anything exists at all is astonishing. The patterns that generate growth, symmetry, and renewal are so reliable that I've stopped noticing how strange and marvelous they truly are. If the heart of magic isn't hand waving, but the continual emergence of life from underlying higher logic, then nature isn't separate from magic. It is the ongoing expression of it.

2. Evolution moves through communication.

Biology describes evolution as variation and selection. But life does not evolve in isolation. Organisms sense pressure, respond to their surroundings, cooperate, compete, and adapt in feedback with the world around them. Evolution is like a conversation—pressure speaking, life responding. Whether that implies a higher intelligence, I can't prove. But given the patterns of communication I've observed in nature, variation and selection alone no longer feel like a complete explanation.

3. Pressure is evolutionary fuel.

Suffering is not evidence of a broken system. It is a signal that something must adjust. When pressure exceeds capacity, discomfort arises. When this pressure is met, equalized, and integrated, it moves the story of life—and each of our stories—toward higher vitality and creative expression. On every scale I can observe, strain precedes strengthening. Even death appears less like failure and more like reset within a larger cycle.

4. Consciousness is fundamental.

Consciousness is often described as a byproduct of an evolved nervous system. But I've begun to see it differently, as the greater context in which life takes shape. Not confined to the brain or produced by the body, but the larger field from which both arise. When I look at the world through this lens, awareness no longer feels isolated inside human skulls but rather woven through the fabric of experience itself. Consciousness, then, is not something we possess. It is something we participate in. From that participation, everything else unfolds.

I didn't arrive at these as claims to defend, but as insights forged through sustained inquiry. I tested them against reason and experience, and kept only what endured. Through this process, I began to see that wisdom is not the possession of answers, but the discipline of remaining open long enough for truth to clarify itself.

Inevitably, I arrive at a simple conclusion: Magic is real.

Magic is why I've always been transfixed by nature's creations, from the geometry on a turtle's back to the feeling of wind across my face. It has been working all along, quietly shaping my life through elemental forces—water carving canyons and blood flowing through my veins, lightning striking forests and sparks racing through my nerves—unfolding even when I wasn't paying attention.

I simply hadn't yet learned how to listen. How to truly see. How to become aware of the consciousness moving through me, and through nature itself.

These realizations only deepen my resolve. I'm not chasing magical powers for myself. I'm wondering. Wandering. Exploring the truly possible. I want to take part in a future that feels bright and alive—not defined by light versus dark, but by integration. By deeper creativity. By fuller expressions of life.

At its essence, magic isn't about egoic control. It's about coherence, emergence, and love. About learning to live in rhythm with the intelligence that shapes all things. And, if we choose, to co-create with that intelligence.

And with that shift…

I start taking Meghan's obsession with crystals a lot more seriously. One night, she places a piece of amethyst on my bedside table. I don't expect much. But something softens in my breath, and I fall into the deepest sleep I've had in weeks.

III: FLIGHT

Amid these insights, I start to understand that the magic of consciousness is actually at least part of the answer I was seeking. It's what ties everything together—the voice, the visions, and the love.

But quickly a new question emerges, now distilled and sharpened:

Where exactly is the portal between consciousness and nature?

I know there is an intersection, a point where the unseen

touches the visible and creates nature. A medium where the magic actually happens.

But where do I find it?

For me, the idea that nature is magical is not enough. I don't want another theory that explains. I want a direct encounter. Something undeniable. Something that leaves me with the deep confidence that I've tracked the truth all the way to the source. To go beyond thought, I know I need to see its power in action, with my own eyes.

But alongside that yearning, more practical matters press in once again. It's becoming increasingly hard to do my job. Teaching basic movement starts to feel repetitive, even hollow. I want to guide people beyond physicality and into something deeper, more integrated, and transformative. I want to show them how movement can be a bridge to nature's role as a teacher, a mirror, and a path to profound evolution.

But when I offer even hints at something deeper, I'm mostly met with disinterest. They came for movement. Not nature as a spiritual teacher. I try to meet them where they are, but inside, I'm growing fatigued. I can't force them towards something that isn't wanted.

I go through the motions. I offer welcoming smiles. I try to remember the beauty in teaching movement for its own sake. I give the attendees what they came for. But in my heart, I'm miserable. Jaded.

As a teacher, it feels excruciating to hold back what I know could illuminate and empower. This isn't just information—it's enlightenment. And keeping it in feels like betrayal.

But I quickly learn that even beyond the movement community, very few people are interested in this enlightenment. Those who are interested in spirituality already have deeply-held beliefs, forged by doctrine, reinforced by ritual, shaped by the structures of religion and the words of man. And newer understandings have already been scooped up and recycled into existing religious proofs.

There's no hunger for something raw and untethered. No readiness to face the unknown, frameless and unnamed.

Not yet, anyway.

The tension I feel inside eventually comes to a head. It's not just the mismatch in teaching. There are internal conflicts within the company, disagreements at the ownership level, and issues far beyond my own personal struggles. But the more I sit with it, the more I begin to see it all as a reflection of what I can no longer tolerate in myself.

After a heated discussion with the owner, I talk it over with Meghan. We both know it's time. I send the resignation email, and that branch of my path comes to its end.

I'm left in a turbulent financial state. But strangely, I feel light. There's no clear plan, no guaranteed income, but we both trust the direction.

I launch a new company: *Spiritual Performance*. The intention is simple and clear: coaching for those seeking a deeper relationship with nature, and by extension, with themselves. Meghan helps me shape the insights I've gathered into an elemental framework: Fire, Water, Earth, and Air, each force representing an essential phase of the journey. I enroll a few clients. It's a decent start.

And despite the instability, one continued practice keeps me centered: going out into nature. That space becomes my clearing ground. Every time I return, I feel emotionally reset, mentally clear, and filled with something deeper than optimism. I feel attuned.

Working with my clients is meaningful, but it carries weight. Guiding people into nature to face their struggles helps some of them. The elemental framework gives structure that proves useful for some. But over time, I begin to see limits. My way isn't for everyone. Many people need stronger stabilizers—religion, community, long-standing social networks—to support deep change. My offering doesn't fit cleanly into any of those models. Nor does the one-on-one coaching model I've been using.

I start to lose clients, and frustration creeps in. Something about my identity as a teacher begins to morph into something I can't yet pinpoint. I feel caught between what I know to be true and what I can practically offer to the world. I'm suspended in the middle, unsure of what's forming, but unable to return to what was. The uncertainty isn't just philosophical. It's financial.

Meghan is supportive through it. She starts teaching again to help make ends meet, and she finds satisfaction in the clearly defined role, structure, and rhythm. Meanwhile, I'm learning how to navigate something much less defined and far more uncertain.

When I go out into nature, I stop wandering freely and instead bring my business challenges with me. I stop leading with wonder and curiosity and start urgently seeking solutions. Ideas keep popping into my head, but they're coming from my ego mind, attempting to turn every insight into a profit-making venture. It feels impure, like a misuse of my questing time.

I start to feel like I'm failing financially, socially, and spiritually. My messages grow desperate. My friends drift away. No one seems to understand what I'm building, or why it matters at all. I start looking into marketing, thinking maybe I just need structure or some proven method for my effort to flow into and yield better results. Something that can make my offerings more palatable, understandable, and enticing. It feels disingenuous, but I convince myself I'm just trying to make what I offer valuable to others. The word I keep encountering in the marketing world is *relatable.*

Relatable? I live off the grid. My passion is roaming in nature.

*My friends are trees and rocks. I refuse any structure or doctrine. I'm
never going to be relatable.*

Each day, the financial pressure mounts, and I'm at a total
loss for what to do about it. I've never felt so helpless in my life.

What am I going to do?

I start applying for jobs. For months, nothing comes through.
I've given so many years to the fitness industry, but it's a solitary
path. Making a living requires working at a gym or becoming an
online influencer. I have no gyms nearby. And I have no desire to
become a fitness influencer once again. I left that world behind.

Finally, something comes through: A local winery needs a
driver and server. The pay isn't great, but it's better than nothing.
In a way, it's a huge relief. It's an easy job that gets me out into
the community. And most importantly, it buys me time to build
my business in a slower, more sustainable way.

It also gives me space to grow personally. I start to see that I
still have a lot more learning and maturing to do before I'm truly
ready to take flight. The "build the plane as you fly it" mentality
clearly wasn't working. And deep down, I get the sense that my
calling isn't to be a coach, at least not in the conventional sense.
I can carry forward the *spirit* of a teacher, but my offering needs
to be something completely fresh.

Time starts to flow more smoothly. I'm no longer in a panic.
I find it genuinely rewarding to channel my natural warmth and
care toward guests coming to the winery. I start to see the wine
as an offering from the land, a kind of plant medicine. And I
enjoy drinking it too. It settles me and softens my ambition. It
reminds me of how to *be*.

Driving also turns out to be unexpectedly nourishing. It taps
into my love of road trips, cruising with the windows down,
listening to music, and contemplating life. I start hearing omens

in the lyrics of songs. I begin noticing angel numbers, like 11:11, appearing constantly, reminding me that I am still on the trail.

The winery grounds me in the local rhythm. I get to know the people of this place, their stories and struggles. I share some of my own and begin to enjoy the soft hum of everyday connection. It's a quiet kind of nourishment. Simple. But very real.

To top it off, my son flies out to visit for the first time. We camp and fish in Colorado. Climb trees. Wander the desert. Read bedtime stories in his new room. He takes to this place immediately, like it's already part of him. He feels the rhythm and adapts with ease.

Even with the wreckage of my failed venture smoldering behind me, I still feel like I'm flying.

Maybe not in the worldly plane. But in spirit, I'm soaring.

IV: CURRENT

THE CURRENT ISN'T something I create but something I return to. A quiet trail already in place, woven into the land, the wind, and the rhythms of this off-grid life I've chosen.

I had tried to fly before I was rooted. Now, back at ground level, I feel the current under my feet once again. Meghan and I settle deeper into our days. Chopping wood. Watering trees. Watching the sun trace its arc across the mesa. Cheering for rainbows after monsoon season rains.

The rhythms of the homestead shape us slowly, like wind carving stone, and we envision how we want to transform it into a thriving ecosystem. It's honest work. Humbling in all the right ways, gratifying, harmonizing. And as the noise of ambition quiets, I start to hear things I'd missed before.

The land is still teaching me. But now, I'm listening differently.

I venture out into the wilderness often, especially during

the warmer months. Each excursion brings something new: an unexplored canyon, a fresh spiritual insight, a deeper sense of the labyrinth that lives in the land behind our home.

My movement practice begins to shift. For a long time, I had dismissed anything that didn't seem obviously useful in the wild, including yoga. I saw it as too controlled, restrictive, and unnatural to enhance my ability to navigate the landscape. But when I began working on my flexibility, something changed: My body opened, and so did my mind. I started to see movement not just as utility, but as expression. As art, like the tiles of the life-force goo I saw in my visions. As a way of honoring the divine intelligence that lives within, setting it free.

With that freedom came a new way of moving in nature. I began to experiment, trying unfamiliar patterns, spirals, and arcs. I stopped moving *over* nature as an obstacle and started dancing *with* it, sharing and co-creating the experience. It brought me back to my martial arts days, when fluidity and angles mattered just as much as structure and force. Less technique, more feel.

Meghan reminds me of my feline nature—Leo the lion as my sun sign. She tells me to watch our cats, who walk the perfect balance between agility and complete relaxation. They hold both tension and ease, motion and stillness. I take her words seriously. I start leaning into my ability to just chill and sleep on my days off. It feels right. Familiar. Like returning to my natural tendencies from childhood.

This perspective helps me reconnect with reading. Less heavy philosophy this time, more stories. I start reading more fantasy, decoding the messages hidden in plain sight. I revisit old favorites: *Lord of the Rings*, *The Alchemist*, and Tom Brown's stories about Grandfather. From this new vantage point, having walked through so many spiritual initiations, I understand them more clearly now.

I also discover new stories, like the *Earthsea* trilogy, written by a Libra—an air sign. The magic in that world is quiet but powerful, rooted in the sacred balance of life. The book is about confronting one's own shadow and stepping into true power—the equilibrium of nature—that serves the whole. I recognize something in that story, a whisper of my own deeper mission.

Finally, I start watching more movies. For a time, I had stepped away from them, dismissing them as mindless entertainment. But with this more integrated, chilled-out perspective, I see the same threads of truth in this visual form of storytelling.

I rewatch some of my old favorites: *The Edge*, *A River Runs Through It*, and *Legends of the Fall*. I see them differently now. Stories of men wrestling with the primal forces of the wild. Stories where passion and beauty are braided with confrontation and madness. Stories where deep inner drives struggle to emerge into the full light of life.

And finally, I rewatch an old favorite from way back in my childhood: *The Never Ending Story*. It's a quest of the highest order, one I hadn't fully understood until now. A journey to restore the value of something pure and deep, yet hiding in plain sight: imagination.

The lyrics of the theme song speak of turning around and seeing the mirror of your dreams in "her face." With all I've come to understand about nature as a living force of magic, I hear it differently now from when I was a kid. *Her face*, I realize, is nature. And nature is the mirror of our dreams. It reflects what we long for, what we fear, what we've forgotten.

The song is about how dreams are everywhere, hidden, yet in plain sight. And how they are the answer to a never-ending story. The lyrics feel like a revelation…one I can't yet fully wrap my mind around. Like a hidden scripture, laced with imagery of nature—clouds, rainbows, dreams, stars. Something about it feels aligned with the essential truth I've been reaching toward all along. As if it holds the answer to my most profound spiritual searching. A thread, still just out of reach, but unmistakably real.

All of it—all I've seen, read, questioned, and felt—is building toward something. I don't know exactly what, but I feel like I'm close to it. There's a pressure forming in the landscape, a whisper behind the wind. As if the land is pulling me toward the grand teaching that will weave all the threads I've been tracking into a tapestry I can finally see.

I don't plan it. I just know that it's time to go out. Time to follow the current to its source.

✦ ✦ ✦

I'm walking up onto the ridge behind my house. From the top, I can see the *Yebbitz* in the distance, about a mile away. The silhouette of their black basalt slabs is sharpened by the white sandstone cathedrals beyond, likening them to altars.

The sun is blazing overhead, high in its summer arc. I sling off my pack and take a few swigs from my water bottle. I'm not sure where I'm going exactly, but I can feel it already: This will be another powerful spiritual adventure.

I drop into the wide sandy wash, following fresh coyote tracks. The path twists and turns, and the sand makes for slow, heavy walking. Between the heat and the exertion, I start scanning the land for shade.

When I reach the base of the *Yebbitz*, I spot a cave near the top and start climbing toward its mouth, craving the coolness. The shadow pulls me in like a promise. The light dose of mushrooms I had taken back at home begins to stir my senses. My focus sharpens. Colors grow more vivid. Edges glint. The land feels subtly alive, responding.

As I step into the cave, I'm met with a natural seat shaped by the rock itself, positioned like a throne facing a basalt wall washed in mineral pastels. Swirls of soft pink, ochre, turquoise, and rust paint the stone like ancient breath.

It feels like an invitation. I set down my pack, take a breath, and settle into the seat. The basalt has that same cryptic code stamped into it, and the face of the stone forms a circular shape, like a target.

I've never done my trance work while gazing into stone, I think to myself.

I pull another plant medicine from my bag—a favorite *rapé*, prepared by a South American tribe. My most trusted ally for open-eyed meditative trance work.

I begin with an offering. First to the earth, sprinkling some onto the cave floor. I ask the medicine to bridge the gap between the land it came from and this sacred land. Then I offer some to the air, blowing it gently toward the mouth of the cave and into the wind.

May this offering fuse the wisdom of the medicine with that of this enchanted land.

Then I load the self-applicator and take a strong dose. I straighten my spine, align my head, and breathe. The *rapé* hits fast and hard, a stiff dose of earthiness that quiets the excitement of my mind.

I fix my gaze on the center of the target. Within moments, it begins to move. The patterns shift, morphing into the face of a woman, then a goat. The color magenta appears again, pulsing like a guide, and draws my gaze upward. The cryptic form in the rock begins to rise from the surface. And then, slowly, it starts to move toward me, closing the distance between the stone and my face.

It penetrates me, seeping directly into my mind's eye. I close my eyes and I finally see the pattern clearly. It's the fleur-de-lis, a flower-shaped symbol of royalty, beauty, and purity that I recognize from one of Meghan's tattoos. I stare in awe, so transfixed that I'm thoughtless.

The symbol begins to shift, morphing into a stunning magenta butterfly. The same one I've often seen during my close-eyed meditations, but now in definition so high it looks more real than life itself.

I open my eyes and I'm stunned by what I see. All the walls of the cave are filled with magenta butterflies, gently flapping their wings. Their presence is overwhelming in the most beautiful way. A memory flashes: I'm back in Kentucky. That place, that feeling. I'm flooded with an emotion I can only describe as reverence. Awe. Sacred knowing.

The butterflies are in everything now, even in my own skin, moving with a soft, flowing grace. When I close my eyes again, they gather gently in my mind's eye.

And from that, I understand.

This is the truth I've been tracking.

It is God—the mind that imagines everything into existence.

In the quiet that follows, an insight rises:

One way I can understand God is as The Dreamer.

The Dreamer is the intelligence behind nature.

Nature is The Dreamer's body—its imagination crystallized into form.

Through leaf, river, creature, and constellation, it experiences itself.

I press my hand against the cool stone to ground myself. After a few breaths, a quiet affirmation rises:

This is it. The moment I've been seeking.

I've finally seen the bridge.

I've glimpsed into the creative portal—the place where consciousness becomes nature.

Nature's magic crystallizes in my mind, not as theory, but as something I've witnessed.

It's as if I see the roots of the tree I've been climbing all along.

It was as simple as asking the right question…and letting it breathe.

Then I hear the voice within:

"This is a pivotal moment, Danny. Now go celebrate."

ETHER

AFTER SUCH A profound epiphany, I expect my life to transform overnight. I imagine clarity, ease, and accelerated progress of some sort. Instead, I find only silence.

Days stretch into months, and with the passage of time, my excitement fades. What was once a burst of clarity now feels like a distant hum, and my energy begins to wane. I keep waiting restlessly for another realization, for a sign, for the next section of my trail to unveil itself.

But nothing comes.

The silence deepens, and the weight of it settles in. I wonder if I've missed something, or if this is all pointless. The light of my revelation blinds me, revealing knowledge, but nothing concrete or actionable.

What good is this knowledge if it doesn't burn through the layers of myself, illuminating a clear path forward? I yearn for a way to enact the wisdom through an offering to the world, but I can't wrap my mind around the fact that I still may have a mountain to climb. I can't see past the glare of my own self—my mind's illusion that I'm on the summit. My ego's craving for something impressive to show for the pinnacle I've reached.

My frustration mounts, tighter and tighter, until it collapses inward, leaving nothing but a deep, suffocating void of sadness. Helplessness settles in, and I feel like a cog in a machine, endlessly spinning, never really able to break free from the imposed structure of society. The weight of the world presses down, and I question whether spiritual wisdom really matters at all. Either way, it seems I'm just another casualty of a system that doesn't care.

I spend the bulk of my day slumped on the couch, watching the dust motes as they hang in the air around me. I find myself pleading to them, begging for a hint at what I should do next. Instead of just enjoying the beauty, I'm feeling desperate and lost.

I think of *The NeverEnding Story*, haunted by "the Nothing," a culture bereft of belief in anything deeper and higher than self and society. I imagine a more primal world, a place where people struggling in the chaos of society could have been a figure of great value. In a spiritually aware culture grounded in nature, such as those found in indigenous populations, each of our passions may have found a more altruistic purpose.

But I know now that looking backward won't fix anything. It's a fantasy to imagine tribal society as just peaceful and idyllic. We can't return to the past, anyway. I've seen where that train of thought leads. The way forward is not a regression, but a new path that expands our limiting narrative toward a greater, more integrated one.

The grief and restlessness shift into a spark of fire deep within, urging me to break free. Helplessness transforms into a burning desire to act, a force ready to erupt. I find myself pushing hard against old beliefs, dissolving the walls of my mind. I'm confronted with the urge to finger-point and lash out, in an effort to forcefully burn through others' barriers. But I know force won't bring freedom.

True freedom lies in channeling this inner friction toward something purposeful, aligned with nature. And, if there's one thing I've learned, it's that nature moves slowly. The real challenge isn't the world outside; it's cultivating understanding and patience within myself. Can I channel my pent-up anger with integrity without letting it consume me?

The urge to lash out becomes a call to refine my energy. I turn to music—once an ally to my athletic pursuits, now a vessel to transmute my anger into something more. I find myself resonating deeply with certain songs, their intensity aligning with the fire burning inside. Specifically, "Aerials" by System of a Down, about losing the *small mind* to free one's life. And "What If" by Creed, an anthem of breaking free from the poison of society's twisted ethos.

Listening to these songs, although they'd spawned from a time of rebellion, has become an almost daily ritual for me. I tap into the raw friction of my struggle, releasing it as fire in my body, as the lyrics echo my own battle for direction. Created in the 1990s, a time when resistance to the synthetic, disembodied vibes of the 1980s was at its peak, these songs speak a language of raw truth, embracing the struggle, forging fires of transformation, and finding a new path of meaning in the storm.

As I listen, this language becomes a form of modern scripture, mirroring my internal struggle. Later, I would discover that both lead singers are Leos—fire signs like myself. I recognize the same blazing spirit in them that I'm learning to cultivate and orchestrate in my own soul.

I channel the spark of rage into my wisdom quests, pushing my body and mind further than ever before. My fitness soars, which is exhilarating, but still reminiscent of my old mindset in wrestling. Soon, I overdo it and quickly feel drained by the intensity. The raw energy quickly becomes unsustainable; my body aches, my spirit wears thin.

Over time, with each quest, the rage naturally settles. It cools, like a red-hot forge transforming into a more steady, golden flame. My fire becomes more focused, and I finally feel less restless, more ready to tune in with less rage and more patience to continue learning.

✦ ✦ ✦

One day, as I walk up the sandy wash toward the *Yebbitz*, I feel the familiar pull of the cave. It's become a ritual, this return to darkness seeking truth. To let silence speak what words cannot. Today, the cave directs me upward into the labyrinth of white sand cathedrals. I'm being summoned to a place called the Heart Chamber, where I can only hope some deeper illumination awaits.

Long before I came to this land, an older man wandered these deserts, carving caves into the compacted white sand formations. But these weren't mere holes in the ground. They were works of art: arches and spirals, vaulted ceilings punctuated by skylights that let the sun stream into the earth. His creations, too wild and beautiful to be embraced, were eventually buried, filled in by officials who feared liability if they ever collapsed. A hidden brilliance, sealed away.

Even half-buried, the remnants still hold their magic. The Heart Chamber calls to me from the highest point in the white sandstone formations. I've been meaning to return. It feels like a sanctuary of fire, where clarity, courage, and inner direction might reignite.

As I approach the frilled formations, the wash splits. The path is unfamiliar, but I've been in this situation before. At the fork, I lift both hands and feel. My right hand pulses with a clear signal. It worked more than once when I was lost, and I trust it again. I veer right.

The wash narrows and twists, the white walls blinding in the sun. I squint and slow down, trying not to overheat. On my left, a thin trail snakes up the ridge, marked with animal tracks. That must be the way.

The first time I came here, it was with a friend—someone effortlessly intuitive, often stumbling into magic. But I wasn't paying attention back then, distracted by conversation. I didn't imprint the route. Now I rely on inner guidance to orient myself and begin the climb.

The ridge is one of many fingers reaching toward the knuckles of the towering sandstone cathedral. The way is steep and broken. Deep crevices demand leaps of faith. I stop often to catch my breath. There was a time I would have pushed through with brute force. But I've learned to honor my body's rhythm. I pause to let the acid flush from my legs and appreciate the view.

Moving through raw land like this is a distinct type of training—dynamic, primal, complete. I realized this back in college, sprinting up the wooded canyons of the Shenandoah with a friend. We'd leap from boulder to boulder along the stream bed. Our muscles burned more after this than a Division I weightlifting session. And we were left with higher levels of agility that made us feel light.

As I climb I think about how nature is now my gym. It is my dojo, my sanctuary. That shift away from the gym was a way of steering my fire toward devotion instead of conquest. Truth isn't just changing how I think. It's changing how I *move*. How I spend my body's energy. Choosing the land more often than the weight room has been a quantum leap, not just in health but in purpose.

At the base of the cathedrals, the incline spirals upward, hugging the white formations. One stretch looks like an ancient staircase, narrow steps etched into the cliffside. To the right, a sheer drop. One misstep could mean death. I wonder if, like in *Aladdin*, the land itself tests intention, if a heart misaligned would cause the stairs to crumble, devouring the intruder.

I traverse carefully, leaning into the wall, whispering to the land that I mean no harm and that I come in reverence. The way finally widens. I exhale. I feel like Indiana Jones, navigating trial after trial, passing through the gauntlet between myself and the treasure.

At the top, I spot the small opening in the side of the formation that is the entrance of the cave. Kneeling at the threshold, I take a deep breath and offer a silent prayer—a plea for clarity, a request for guidance. Then I enter.

I have to keep my head down to avoid hitting it on the ceiling. If the sand hadn't been backfilled, I'd be able to walk with a few inches of clearance over my head. The backfill gives the space a forbidden air, like a dusty forgotten temple, a place of spirits, secrets, and treasures.

The coolness of the cave embraces me, soothing my heated body. I rest against a pillar with a serpent carved into the surface and allow my gaze to soften. I let the stillness of the space cool my fire, letting my energy settle, just for a moment. But after a while, I begin to feel a chill. My body is craving the warmth of the sun. Time to step back out into the light. I plan to climb to the top of the formation and enjoy the view.

As I walk toward a spot where I can climb upward, I notice another tiny entrance. I stick my head in to see a chamber barely big enough for me to fit inside. There's an exit on the other side, so I climb in. In a far corner, I notice a bit of black canvas fabric sticking up from under the sand.

I give the corner of the canvas a tug, pulling back the sand to reveal something buried beneath. I reach in and feel something solid. Stone, cool to the touch. I pull it into the light and examine it. It's a white statue, its form incomplete like a melted candle, flame-shaped yet undefined. My inner voice speaks softly:

This is a representation of The Dreamer: the dancing, etheric flame. Not just raw fire, but integrated wholeness before it descends into creation.

I recognize what the statue represents immediately, bolstered by my plant medicine experiences. I think of the goo I saw in my visions, creating form through art before solidifying into Earth. Carrying the statue, I climb to the top of the formation. With the vast land stretched out before me, I feel my fire aligning with the world around me. This is the place where passion and purpose converge, lifting the lower octaves of rage into higher notes of devotion.

I close my eyes and think about how I am ready to serve nature, to help bring hidden spiritual truth into the light and guide others with the fire that moves through me. I surrender my will to the flow of creation, trusting that the Dreamer knows the way, and that nature will show me how to use my fire well.

My purpose is not mine alone. It belongs to something greater.

As that inner declaration settles, something shifts within, like a key turning in a lock. I feel it: an invisible threshold crossed.

Then I hear a voice, clear and profound:

"My son, you are ready to do wonderful things. Your fire has carried you far and high. But now, you must see things from my perspective: the God's-eye view. I am your higher self. And you are me.

"Now, open your eyes and admire your creation. Not just mine. Yours. All of ours."

I open my eyes and let the words settle, not as revelation but as remembrance. I am not separate from creation—it is an extension of my very being. And I, an extension of it. I look out at the land and see it with new eyes, as my own masterpiece, here and now. And more than that. My child. Alive, breathing, growing. Needing care.

"You're so beautiful," I whisper in a steady voice. My heart swells with warmth and love. I place my hands on my chest, feeling the heat of purpose rising. I move my hands away from my chest, sending the light outward. I imagine it moving through the land, the air, the water, the fire.

And then, to my surprise, I feel it pouring back into me. It makes me feel lighter, more energized. Pure, radiant. Amplified.

I feel like the sun—bright, steady, and devoted to giving. And in that clarity, something deeper emerges: The part of creation, of the cosmos, that is mine to tend to is the Earth. The Earth is mine to help grow, not through ownership but through offering my light. My flame is not meant for my own glory. It's meant for *giving*. For *brightening* and serving the living field of creation.

I make a vow, now directly to the Earth: I will offer my fire in service of creation in whatever way I can. I affirm this both inwardly and outwardly as a solemn promise to the land, to the life that moves through it, to the greater cosmic dream it's enfolded within.

I look up toward the sun and feel its steady warmth. It fills me with hope. I see now what I couldn't before:

Despite its power, the sun does not shine for praise. It shines for nature, illuminating, and warming the world to elevate it from a state of coldness to happiness and joy.

And, as I discovered, when I give my power to the Earth even with a simple gesture, it gives it right back, amplified and restructured in a way that somehow restores my own inner light. It's like a dance, an endless cycle of self-perpetuating power. The energy I offer the Earth becomes part of something greater instead of a drain, wasted on anger and misdirected force. And the light the Earth returns to me rejuvenates my mind and strengthens my body. The burnout I once felt was never from the fire itself. It came from aiming it in the wrong direction.

Now I understand:

True power is aimed power. Not aimed at egoic radiance, burning for oneself. Not aimed at the smoky fire of rage, burning to destroy. Power aimed at serving the Earth and all of its creations is ethical. For Earth's purpose is infusing fire into form, coloring the world, manifesting the dream of nature. Aligning myself with the Earth is how I learn how to wield my fire.

I rise and begin the journey home. But every step is different now. Each one is a devotional act—a quiet rhythm offered back into the pulse of creation.

In the days that follow, I feel my fire begin to shift. It no longer burns to fight. I don't reject the warrior within who once chased glory, who wanted to wage war on the world. That fire still burns from a deep place, echoing the power from the first sparks and ferocity of my youth. I can always call on it for protection, if needed. But now I've learned I have to continually direct my fire to fuel a different kind of warrior: a sun, helping to illuminate the Earth for the glory of creation.

Even if I don't yet know exactly how to best serve the Earth, I now understand that it can start with a simple gesture, with the intention of giving.

I'm not here to wage war. I'm here to help light the way.

11: RIVER

I had gained a higher vantage, sworn an oath of service, and begun walking in conscious unity with nature. After learning how to be more sun-like, I believed clarity would carry me forward. I expected inspiration to come easily now, with new and better ways to contribute to creation unfolding organically.

But once again, life had other plans.

The clarity I once felt under the sun began to dissolve, softening into something quieter, more complex. The lofty expectations I'd placed on that revelation gave way to a slower, heavier current. I found myself caught in emotional turbulence. Feelings rose and crashed without warning. I expected more power and encountered the opposite.

Some days were exhilarating, lifting me with bursts of perspective and purpose. Others pulled me under, leaving me heavy and unsure. At times I spiraled into dark trains of thought, searching the internet, convinced I was sick, delusional, or destined to fail. My body ached as if something unseen were pressing down on me, testing for weakness.

I felt especially exposed when trying to share my perspective with others. Friends drifted away. Family members openly challenged my beliefs. Even spiritual allies seemed to vanish. My work stalled. Coaching clients thinned. I felt more alone than I ever had.

I tried to fight the riptide. Caffeine to lift my mood. Wine to dull the stress. I doubled down on positive thinking, exercise, meditation—anything to shift the tide. But nothing held. The more I tried to override the heaviness, the deeper I sank. Physical discomfort fed mental irritation, and the irritation made rest impossible. Even when I knew a nap might help, I reached instead for stimulation, grasping for any sort of control.

One day, Metallica came on the radio, and the lyrics of "Sad but True" voiced what I couldn't yet say aloud: Something below the surface was controlling my thoughts and actions, desperately trying to help me avoid the pains of life.

I kept questing into nature, hoping to reset, but returned drained. I began to wonder if I had done something wrong and now creation had turned away from me. Even the land seemed silent.

Then, I had a flash of insight: I had learned to focus my fire through Earth. But my water still ruled me. No matter how hard I tried to stay elevated and helpful, I kept sinking, unable to even help myself. I spiraled into exhaustion, loneliness, frustration, and doubt. It felt like my own soul was divided: one half trying to rise and the other pulling me down.

Eventually, something broke open. I stopped chasing insight and reframed the quest entirely. Instead of wandering into nature hoping to climb my way into clarity, I chose to go with a more humble intention: to enter the landscape as a student of water. To learn how to navigate the weight instead of always reaching for the sky. To understand how to flow.

✦ ✦ ✦

I'd been meaning to visit this river valley nestled high in the southern Rockies of New Mexico. Though it's only an hour from home, the energy here feels entirely different. The short, curvy desert junipers and piñon pines give way to towering alpine fir and sharp-needled spruce. The air is crisp and clean, and the land speaks in cooler, darker tones. The deep greens and blues of the forest welcome me in; the river sings a whimsical song.

I sling on my backpack and head down the trail that follows the river's edge. The high-altitude terrain here feels softer than the Rockies in Colorado. A bit gentler, more forgiving. Butterflies dance among the trees. An etheric quality hangs in the air, as if this is a confluence of worlds.

The trail winds gently into a canyon, and my mind begins to sing with the rhythm of the land. I glide along, my feet connecting to the earth through thin hiking sandals. The forest's sweet yet crisp aroma fills my lungs. I revel in the newness of it all. After the mental heaviness I've been trapped in, this optimism feels like sunlight breaking through fog.

Soon, I reach a sheer rock face that forces me across a wooden bridge to the opposite bank. The trail becomes steeper, rockier. As I ascend into an aspen grove, the contrast between the pale trunks and dark soil stirs something in me. Without thinking, I break into a sprint, childlike and free, as if I'm in a dream where exhilaration reigns and sadness doesn't exist.

As I climb, the mood shifts. The forest thickens and darkens, slowing my pace. A tiny fairy stream, as Meghan calls them, crosses the path. A boulder catches my eye, inviting me to rest. I crouch beside it, catching my breath and wondering what lies just beyond the view of the trees.

I spot a narrow deer trail winding downhill and follow it. As

I descend, I notice black eye-like knots in the aspen bark watching me. I can't tell if they approve, but I feel welcome enough to continue.

The trail fragments into a maze. I swap paths again and again, unsure if I'll be able to find my way back. The joy I'd felt starts to unravel into subtle fear. The forest darkens further and starts to feel foreboding. I consider turning around, but my body keeps moving forward. Slowly, the fear loosens its grip, and I begin to trust again.

The woods open into a clearing. For the first time since moving to New Mexico, I see the ground blanketed in clover. The word *lucky* echoes in my mind. From here, I glimpse the broad sweep of the valley, encased by wide-shouldered rock formations. I sense the river nearby and feel a pull, like it's drawing me to something sacred.

At the end of the clearing, I re-enter a patch of forest. The trail narrows again, easy and effortless beneath my feet. I slow my pace at a set of boulders stacked like steps leading downward, sensing I've arrived somewhere important.

I feel a twinge of sheepishness, like I've stumbled into a holy place. I pause, fill my heart with reverence, and silently ask the land for permission to enter. Instantly, I feel lighter. My pace quickens. I begin to notice flat, smooth river stones beneath my feet, some of them shaped like hearts. A quiet certainty settles over me: I'm where I need to be.

As I pass through a thick line of trees, the ground sparkles with bits of mica glinting in the sunlight. I feel a warm, elated buzz move through my body.

A breeze stirs. Thick, grey clouds begin to gather, dimming the light as I reach the riverbank. I sit beneath a tree beside a slow-spinning eddy, beyond which crystal-clear water giggles over the rocks.

The eddy spins gently, yet remains mostly transparent. Beneath the surface, a gnarled tangle of roots jut from the bank. A dark hole at their base disappears into the tree's trunk. I laugh, noting the unmistakable resemblance to female anatomy. From the black muck beneath, delicate green vines rise toward the water's surface.

Lying on my stomach with my hands propping up my head, I gaze into the swirl. A thin, oil-like iridescent film shimmers on the surface. It's as if I'm peering into the raw ingredients of life itself—dark chaos swirling into flowing forms, colored by sunlight, coalescing into beauty in the current of creation. In my mind, I see water in its many expressions: the serenity of a mineral-blue alpine lake, the quicksilver clarity of a mountain stream, the muddy chaos of a swollen river, the musky thickness of a swamp, and the salt-stung calm of the open ocean.

All water, morphing in texture and color, yet part of one current. Just like my emotions. Just like me. Each state of mind is part of the water cycle that shapes and cleanses me like it does the planet. And when I resist one phase, I dam the flow, impeding the regenerative flow of life. But when I move through them—or rather I allow them to move through me, feelings flowing into feelings—I return to the natural, unimpeded cycle.

Gratitude wells up suddenly like a flood. I sit up, press my hands to my heart, overcome by rapture. The feeling is vast, narcotic, cleansing. For a moment, all pain dissolves. I want nothing. I am whole.

But just as I settle into bliss, the sun vanishes and cold air rushes in. The river loses its sparkle. I feel a chill, and with it, the moment of wholeness slipping away. My muscles contract, shivering, and I'm left worried about myself, wishing the cold would stop violating my system and my newfound peace.

Desperate to recover, I step into the icy river, barefoot, climbing onto a sun-warmed rock. But it's smaller than I thought, barely wide enough for both feet, and not warm at all. I try to summon the sun with my mind like I've done before. A breeze answers, but instead of revealing warmth, it strips the last of it away. The cold pierces me. My body starts to shiver all over. My butt muscles shake violently, threatening my balance. I hunker down on the rock, too proud to retreat, staring into the flowing water and waiting in discomfort.

Then, an image flashes. The armadillo-like creature from my *yagé* vision, curled up, resisting the flow. I remember the message: *uncurl*. Stop resisting, rejecting the discomfort, mentally and physically. Accept it, and allow it to teach and renew me.

I stand, shivering. I surrender to the cold, trusting that something will shift. I imagine the icy bite cleansing my system, like a pristine alpine river. I see myself in a boat, paddle in hand, no longer fearing the complexity and intensity of the current. No longer bracing and curling up in fear of the unknown and uncomfortable. I'm riding the current, trusting my bond with water to help me navigate its ebbs and flows.

And something shifts. The cold moves through me and then… leaves. Warmth returns, not from the sky, but from within. My resistance dissolves. I've let go. Or maybe my pain tolerance has grown. Either way, it feels like relief.

Gratitude swells again, and I feel proud of myself for facing the cold. I bow, silently thanking the river for the lesson. Then, softly, I ask: *Is there a way to call the sun back?*

The answer moves through me like a breeze: *Just ask. From a place of gratitude.*

I close my eyes and fill my heart with thanks—for the water, for its challenge, for its beauty. Then my wrestling career flashes through my mind. The emotional pain. The brutal grind of practice. The suffering of cutting weight. The sting of defeat.

I never won the gold medal I chased. But I see myself standing on a mountain summit, arms outstretched—victorious in a deeper way. Shaped by pressure, forged by hardship, emerging stronger without losing my belief in the beauty of life. I see myself learning to accept challenge and pain without letting them consume me, allowing their weight to shape my raw fire into skills I would carry forward into my life.

I thank my parents and all those who loved and supported me through the lessons of my childhood. My father, Don, for always being in my corner, believing in my power. My mother, Leonora, for modeling self-confidence and honoring my unconventional path. My sister, Sara, for showing me how to go inward and create art from the depths, even when it's misunderstood. And so many others whose support shaped me in ways I'm only beginning to understand. Then I thank myself for my willingness to keep learning, navigating the challenges of relationships, career, and calling.

And with that understanding, I thank the water more fully for its pressure, its teaching, its love. I release any expectation of calling the sun back. I trust the strengthened connection between myself and the water. I know I can't control the outcome. All I can do is ask.

The clouds still hang thick, offering no sign of change. If anything, it looks like rain.

Time stretches. The sky remains gray. But the wind softens. The air feels different—less biting, more awake. A hush settles over the valley. I dissolve into the long dance of time, grateful to be immersed in it despite my preferences, despite the lingering edge of discomfort.

Then a crack of light breaks through. A single beam of sunlight pierces the clouds, laying a golden ribbon across the water. Slowly, it widens. The whole river begins to glow. Stones beneath the surface gleam like treasure. What was hidden becomes revealed in an explosion of light.

The warmth hits my skin. I feel it entering and radiating outward through me. A soft clarity opens in my chest, as though the light is illuminating not just the land, but my very essence.

It feels like a baptism—a rebirth by fire, gifted by water. I realize I don't need to fight away pain as if it were the enemy. The discomfort has a role: to tear me apart and re-sculpt me, healing my cracks and stripping away layers that no longer belong. And steer me down my truth path, as it has so many times before.

I realize that resisting is only prolonging the pain. Sometimes I have to hurt in order to heal. So when I soften and open up, accepting the heaviness, I am placing my ego aside and allowing the current of life to carry me toward my truest expression of self—my contribution to nature's dream.

On the hike back, I reflect on how hard it is to stay open. How quickly my small mind tries to build walls, grasp for ease, and flee discomfort. Why is it so hard to trust the river of life? There must be an easier way.

Before I get into my truck, I return to the river and kneel beside it. I ask if there's something I can carry with me. A simple reminder of what I've learned.

The current murmurs. And then I hear not laughter anymore but words unmistakable and clear. *Thank you,* repeating endlessly.

Thank you, I echo inwardly. Maybe it really is that simple.

I put it to the test. By speaking the words, but also by opening my arms and releasing the feeling of gratitude, as if I were giving nature a hug. I recognize the feelings I am throwing outward as approval and passionate love for creation, for life itself.

Despite pain and grief, gratitude remains accessible. And more than that, a balm for anxiety, allowing me to continue moving forward instead of being stuck in my own eddies of victimhood. Through gratitude, I learn how to better wield my inner water.

I bow to the river. As I walk back to my truck, I realize that gratitude is the most rejuvenating vibration there is. A way of tapping into nature's brilliance, of continually renewing myself, and living in sync with nature's dream.

III: TREES

Time moves forward in a rhythm, an ever-changing dance of light, sky, cloud, and rock. In the high desert, each season carries its own signature of mood, change, and teaching.

I go on periodic wisdom quests into the wilderness, tracking my next steps, but nature reveals my trail through more than just the elements. It speaks in light and form, in the dance between creation and destruction—each track a reflection of its creator's manifold grace.

Meghan and I continue carving out our home base. We tend to the spaces in and around the house, shaping it into a reflection of who we are through painting, planting, arranging, and filling it with treasures gathered from the land. Meghan launches a small online store, offering rocks, resins, and wild plants she collects on our walks. We wander and gather together, receiving these gifts. Sometimes side by side, sometimes alone, each in our own style of communion with the land.

We each continue our work in society. I remain at the winery, delivering libations across the state. I also work with a few coaching clients. But as I go through the motions, I feel a quiet dissonance building. This way of teaching—through screens, calls, and frameworks—no longer feels like the full expression of my soul's work. Meghan shifts her own role, moving from classroom teaching to special education. We're both shedding old skins, searching for work that fits us more honestly.

Still, I keep wondering: *What is my true place in the world? How do I share the teachings of nature if not through coaching? Am*

*I meant to invite others into the wild, to let the land speak for itself?
Or is there another way still waiting to reveal itself?*

Softly echoing in the back of my mind is the awareness that
my own contemplations and questions are still an intricate part
of my tracking. In other words, I can't just passively let nature
lead me; I must actively participate, leading myself with my own
wonder and curiosity.

However, in the absence of clear and immediate answers,
I fall into familiar patterns. Lifting weights to build muscle.
Stretching to stay limber. Reading philosophy to feel progress.
None of it feels inherently wrong, but it all keeps me circling the
same ground. A holding pattern.

I bounce between old routines, feeling untethered but craving structure to fill my days with, and a clear goal to evolve
toward. But I also want to earn an income to support the more
financially abundant lifestyle I once had. I try starting new proj-
ects—online courses, business ideas, all with the intention of
helping the Earth—but nothing sticks. I begin writing a book,
only to abandon it after one chapter.

Insights come easily. My mind keeps generating visions,
revelations, and answers. But instead of integrating them and
allowing them to find their true relevance in my journey, I scram-
ble to turn them into something marketable. Then, one day, a
voice cuts through the mental noise:

*Remember: Not every insight is a business opportunity. Sit with
them. Trust the process.*

The message lands. Despite my devotion, my willingness to
be like a sun, despite my better ability to flow with the river of
life, some deeper part of me is still grasping for something more
tangible and concrete. My small mind still believes it must force
results, shape a product, and prove my worth. It takes the sacred

and tries to package it, measure it, sell it. Not purely out of greed, but out of habit, fear, and a need to matter.

But maybe my urge to create something concrete from the sacred isn't wrong. Maybe there is treasure a bit further down the trail, waiting to be unearthed.

✦ ✦ ✦

I'm walking along an old wagon trail, deep in the desert. The wide, winding sandy path cuts into the side of a mountain, offering a sweeping view of the Rockies to the east. It's a warm spring day, and the landscape sings with freshness and light.

I come across a section where the trail has been eroded by countless flash floods and the entropy of time. I want to head down into the sprawling canyon below anyway, so I take the eroded part of the trail as a cue to work my way downward. Like a mountain goat navigating a steep cliffside, I cut my boots into the clay-rich sand, zigzagging as I carve my descent.

I end up in a tight, snaking wash that's just above my height on either side and barely wide enough for my feet. I pick up my pace to a run, using momentum to leap from side to side with ease. It feels like an obstacle course—like *American Ninja Warrior*—as fallen trees and huge boulders are leapt over, weaved around, and ducked beneath.

The wash gradually widens, so I up my pace again, full-on sprinting now. My body leans forward, jaw clenched, eyes narrowed sharp like a falcon's. I race ahead, feeling the wind whip by as I move with full speed. In my mind's eye I see myself as my son's hero, Sonic the Hedgehog, blazing through the landscape.

Eventually, I reach the main canyon and slow myself down to a walk. I pause and put my hands behind my head, trying to catch my breath. After a few hundred yards of walking and regaining my composure, I spot a beautiful juniper tree offering a cool, shady reprieve from the sun, which combined with the exertion, has made my body dangerously overheat.

I make my way into the shadow of the tree, feel into its cool relief, throw my pack on the ground, and collapse into the sand. Once I regroup myself enough to sit up, I pull out my water bottle and take a long drink.

The cold liquid slides down my throat, and my body buzzes with euphoria as my brain releases pain-killing chemicals. I lie back, letting the coldness of the sand envelop me. When I open my eyes, something dangling in the sunlight above catches my attention: a golden substance oozing from the exposed roots of the juniper tree. The sunlight shines through it, coloring it an almost translucent yellow.

Curious, I sit up to get a closer look. It's slightly sticky but almost solid, like resin. I break off a piece and hold it up to my nose. It smells of citrus and pine. I wash it with some water and taste it. The lemony flavor is bright, but it's muted by a chalky aftertaste. Warm energy pulses within, a sensation of lightness, brightness, and focus. I gather a little more of it and continue on my journey.

Hours later when I arrive home, I show it to Meghan. She's delighted by its beauty and immediately goes outside to search for more in the junipers around our house. She finds some, burns it at her altar, and the air fills with lemon-scented smoke.

"This stuff is really special," she says with reverence and awe. I agree, and wonder for a moment if there's some deeper meaning to this gift I've received from the trees. Unable to find it, I move on, but the bright chalky taste lingers in my memory for weeks, as if the tree had purposely imprinted itself into me.

✦ ✦ ✦

A few months pass by. I'm on another quest, this time guided by the wisdom of the cave at the *Yebbitz*. After consulting with its power, it steers me upward toward a steep boulder field I've never explored before. As I scan the expanse before me, my eyes are drawn to the towering trees scattered throughout, larger and older than any I've encountered before. The contrast between the massive dark grey boulders and the towering trees creates an exotic, almost mystical atmosphere. It's as if I've stumbled upon a forgotten city hidden in the heart of a lost jungle, waiting to reveal its secrets.

As I leave the *Yebbitz*, I follow what appears to be a trail but I soon realize isn't. This is something I've encountered before: No human-made path, just the natural architecture of the land guiding me along a secret route. It leads me into a tight canyon.

The canyon is guarded by smaller junipers with thin trunks stretching and intertwining in all directions, creating a maze that's difficult to navigate. I crawl under and over, sometimes squeezing through tiny openings, twisting and turning, until I finally emerge beyond the junipers and find myself at the end of the canyon and the beginning of the sloped boulder field.

To my left is a colossal juniper tree with a massive trunk as thick as a dinosaur, branches glowing in the sunlight like it's on fire. I stand in awe for a moment, but I'm too focused to linger. I push forward, climbing and weaving my way between the giant boulders, until I reach the top of the field. My body aches as I climb, but I'm unwilling to stop until I've made it to the summit.

When I finally reach the top, I collapse beneath a beautiful bushy juniper tree. Its presence feels grounding and nurturing. Exhausted, I close my eyes and sink into its needly bed. In my daze, I hear a soft voice flowing through me:

"Don't do anything reckless. You aren't ready."

As the fatigue drains from my body, I begin to feel restored.

I open my eyes, stand up, and realize I'm at the top of a mesa. I walk around, taking in the dynamic landscape unfolding before me, my mind still lingering on the voice I heard.

Not ready for what?

I let the thought go and continue onward, captivated by the new terrain. Huge junipers stand tall and sun-bleached dry riverbeds carve through the sloping land in winding arcs. I follow a path that parallels the main wash, which leads me to what seems like stone steps, rising up a small ridge. When I reach the top, I pause in awe.

Ahead, three massive rock formations rise abruptly from the desert floor. They stand only a few yards apart, each jutting at least thirty feet high. The stark white sand background in the distance gives them a saintly, almost noble appearance.

The Three Kings. The formations tell me their names before I even ask.

As I approach, the caution of the bushy juniper tree echoes in my mind. I circle the first formation, studying its vertical face. There's no clear route up. I move to the back of the middle rock, where I spot a series of crevices offering a way. But halfway up, I realize there's nothing left to grab. I carefully descend and turn to the final formation.

This one is less vertical, and I quickly identify a viable route. Within minutes, I reach the top. The view is breathtaking, and I feel emboldened, as if I've absorbed the strength of the rocks themselves. For a brief moment, I feel unstoppable, kingly, immortal.

To my left, I see the tops of the other two formations. It looks like I could jump from where I stand to the middle one. Just as I'm about to leap, the words of the junipers echo once again: *You aren't ready.*

I glance downward at the drop below and suddenly realize

that one mistake and I would certainly fall to my death. My ego protests, egging me on:

You can do it. You've trained for this all your life.

I sit down, forcing myself to pause. For a moment, I allow the inner voices to quiet, letting the gravity of the situation settle in. My old impulsive, fiery self would have surely taken the chance. Especially if I could capture it on film, using it as an advertisement for the movement training I once taught.

But something inside me shifts. I see the temptation for what it is: an unnecessary risk from a low value of my own life. A pursuit of money, fame, and a thrill that overshadows the preciousness of life.

But life itself is what I'm devoted to now, not self glorification. And I must walk the walk, embodying the sun-like perspective I've earned. I must become a living example of that devotion.

I decide not to jump. My ego flares, making me feel as though I'm giving in to fear. But deep within, I know this choice is one of wisdom. I understand that my bruised ego may haunt me for a while, so I make a peace offering: If the jump continues to haunt me, I'll return one day, perhaps with more power or skill to make it safer.

This inner agreement softens me. I descend, feeling triumphant in a way.

As I make my way down, I glance back at the Three Kings. I feel them nodding in approval, as if to say, *good choice.* I laugh softly to myself and nod in return.

When I pass the juniper tree that had warned me, I sit beneath its canopy and thank it for its wisdom. It's a little awkward, as I've never spoken to a tree before, but it feels right. I touch the trunk and bow softly in gratitude before continuing my descent. This time, I decide I'll take a different route down.

I feel near boundless strength and energy as I jump downward from boulder to boulder, navigating another maze of colossal junipers. I can see that water periodically runs down this area, helping the trees grow strong and healthy. But these junipers also look more feminine, their stature more flowing than bulky. Unlike the thick, dinosaur-like one I had seen on the way up, epitomizing virility, these ladies' long limbs exude more flowing vitality, grace, and wisdom.

As I move through them, I hear a voice again:

"Do you believe in immortality?"

Umm, I guess I believe anything is possible, I respond, feeling strange about the question.

"The alchemists believed in immortality. You should look into that field."

I don't really feel called to immortality or turning lead into gold. I believe in the way of nature, and I don't want to tamper with it, I respond.

"That's wise. But it's a mistake to love nature and dismiss this field. Alchemy is the way of nature."

The voice continues, *"Your path has been about fusing human vitality with nature. That's the deeper pursuit of alchemy. It is learning about the art of vitality from nature itself. The fruit of this path is earned through a nature-devoted mindset though, not an ego-devoted one. Which is why the fruit is so seldom cultivated."*

I'll look into it, I agree, despite my initial hesitation. How can I deny such powerful guidance from a tree?

I keep making my way home, but as I pass new trees, new insights keep flowing in, as if each tree is adding its own nugget of wisdom.

"Here's one more hint about vitality: Sexual energy is the key. Not wasting it recklessly, though enjoying it thoroughly. Savoring it. Allowing its energy to become a refined state you are in constantly.

Gradually, you will become aroused by the spirit of life itself. Let this energy deeply nourish, invigorate, and guide you."

I thank the junipers for their wisdom and continue onward. As I trot my way through the desert, I feel my strength and power gradually shifting. The raw energy inside shapes itself into a more fluid, nourishing current. I recognize an erotic energy, and instead of pushing it away, thinking it's the wrong time and place for it, I allow it to rise.

It makes me feel more vibrant and alive and helps me resonate even more powerfully with the beauty of nature. Though the feeling does not last, the taste of it confirms the wisdom of the junipers and leaves a mark upon me.

Over the next few days, I dive into researching alchemy and uncover another hidden pathway into wonder and fresh inspiration. I learn that alchemy is a fusion of science and spirit, grounded in studying the processes of the Earth itself. It is not an abstract cosmology but an investigation of the intelligence of plants, minerals, and metals. My faith in the junipers—and in my own ability to connect with trees—feels validated.

Amid my research, I remember a book I bought years earlier in Vermont: *Evolutionary Herbalism*. At the time, I had no intention of making herbal preparations professionally, but the title had caught my eye.

To my surprise, the book is infused with alchemical principles alongside detailed preparation methods. The alchemists of old considered the soul of a plant to be its essential oil. Curious, I begin exploring research on essential oils and discover a growing body of evidence supporting their benefits when inhaled—and even ingested. Yet the field remains uncertain. Essential oils are powerful substances, not always easily digested or well understood.

Alchemy, however, approaches this challenge differently.

Through careful processes, the purified mineral salts of a plant are recombined with its oil, forming microscopic structures that make the essence easier for the body to absorb.

The deeper I look, the more fascinated I become. Alchemy is not merely mystical speculation; it is the root from which modern chemistry emerged. As a study of nature's intelligence, it feels like a reservoir of untapped potential—for new technologies and deeper understandings of life itself.

Then a golden wave of clarity moves through me.

I realize I've found my craft.

As I immerse myself in alchemical study, I see parallels with martial arts. It will require discipline, patience, and devotion. But unlike the lofty, sun-like perspective I've been living in, this path offers something grounded. Something tangible. A way to shape insight into form.

Whatever I create will not simply be a product made for profit. It will be an offering along the nature-based trail I've been tracking. And if that offering remains rooted in service to the Earth, I trust it will also sustain my own life along the way— not riches, perhaps, but enough to live, love, and participate in nature's dream.

My small mind still whispers worries about money, time, and success. But a deeper pursuit now calls louder. Alchemy will become one of the lenses through which I study and serve the Earth.

I will craft tinctures from plants, minerals, and metals. By studying celestial rhythms and capturing terrestrial essences, I will explore the bridge between heaven and earth.

Suddenly I understand something a wise timber-framing Capricorn friend of mine once told me:

Craft is the remedy.

With alchemy as my craft, I find a clearer direction for my

devotion. Nature no longer flows only into me, but through me—structuring wisdom into form and guiding me toward my highest creative expression.

Like the resin on the juniper tree, I've discovered a way to offer the world something golden.

IV: STARS

I devour everything I can find on alchemy, hungry for knowledge. One foundational axiom stands out above the rest:

As above, so below.

The implication is that nature is woven from repeating patterns, echoing at every scale. The curve of a planet mirrors that of a grain of sand. The moon circling Earth mirrors an electron orbiting an atom. The structure of the cosmos reflects itself within each of its creations.

I begin to see life differently. DNA is no longer the sole creator of life, but a tool—transcribing the intelligence of the Dreamer into form. Nature itself becomes the true temple. Every detail holds a fragment of cosmic design. By studying the small, I can begin to understand the grand.

The principle of correspondence opens another doorway: astrology.

From this perspective, the patterns of the planets and stars offer insight into ourselves and the Earth. For example, I am a Leo sun, meaning my core pattern corresponds to the sun itself, and my primary element is fire. This aligns closely with my personality and disposition.

Meghan is a Sagittarius, which corresponds to Jupiter, and her element is also fire. This explains why we align so well in ethos and mission, and also why we occasionally find ourselves in intense "fire fights."

While Meghan isn't as drawn to the scientific side of alchemy as I am, astrology captivates her completely. For her, astrology becomes an intuitive way to explore the human psyche and how the zodiac signs influence emotional and mental patterns. In a way, the signs are the stars shining through us, each reflecting a unique constellation of psychological forces.

Meghan also connects astrology to natural forms—crystals and resins—and begins using them to elicit specific mental states: energized, relaxed, or focused.

Together, through astrology, we experience a kind of awakening, discovering new ways of seeing and exploring reality—not through blind faith, but through curiosity and experimentation. This deepens our relationship as we begin to understand each other more clearly.

It also begins shaping our respective crafts. For Meghan, as a teacher, astrology becomes a way to better connect with and serve her students. For me, as a student of nature exploring alchemy as a tool, it offers a philosophical foundation—one that may guide how I translate nature's intelligence into formulations that support vitality and performance.

✦ ✦ ✦

Road trips always excite me, and this one is no different. We're headed to Pagosa Springs, Colorado, one of my favorite places. It's early spring, and I'm eager to breathe in the fresh, crisp Colorado air while gazing at the austere snow-covered San Juan Mountains. We'll only be there for a night, but it's worth the trip. Plus, we love the drive. It's our time to connect, philosophize, and process the current events of our lives.

It takes just under three hours to reach the town center, but, as usual, the drive flies by. It's much colder here than at home, but fortunately, there are hot springs. We decide to take a dip and spend a few moments deciding whether to visit the expensive resort in town or the free ones across the river. We choose the free springs, aiming to save our money for a fun night of dining in town before heading up into the mountains to camp.

After changing into our bathing suits in the car, we walk down the paved path toward the river. Just before a bridge, the hot springs announce their presence with rising, swirling steam. We slip into one of the clear, blue-tinged mineral pools, a larger one near the river. Settling into the hot water feels like a warm hug, and the heat instantly melts our muscles into a fully-relaxed state.

Time slows as we unwind, soaking in the magnesium, sulfur, and other therapeutic minerals. Meghan grows too hot and sits on a rock, contemplating whether or not to plunge into the icy waters of the San Juan River. With a deep breath, she goes for it, fully committing to a dive beneath the surface. I'm impressed but not quite ready to follow her lead. Instead, I lean back, staring up at the sky, feeling like life is perfect.

Then, I sense the ripples of another person entering the pool and hear the hurried footsteps and sniffing of a dog. I glance over and see a beautiful husky investigating the area. Sitting across from me in the pool I see a man who could resemble someone in my family with Italian-Irish features similar to mine and warm, inviting eyes. I offer a nod, and he introduces himself with a smile.

"Hey, I'm Rob."

Immediately, I feel a sense of connection with him, as if we've known each other in a past life. We chat for a bit, and eventually, he asks what I do for a living. I tell him I am working at a winery and studying alchemy. He smiles and mentions that he used to teach alchemy.

For real?

After I share my interests, he tells me about his former business, which was centered around alchemical extractions. I'm fascinated but not surprised by this encounter. I know well by now that when we're ready to receive, creation provides.

But there's a mysteriousness to Rob, not just in his character but also in his story. He tells me he's living in the area, camping in the woods full-time. He mentions there's a long story about what happened to his business, and something in his tone suggests it didn't end well. I try to probe gently, but his response is curt, giving me the sense he's not ready to revisit that part of his life. I wonder what really happened, but I don't press him further.

On the car ride home, I tell Meghan about Rob since they had only exchanged a brief wave. "Weird," she says. "He really does look like he could be your brother."

At home, I look Rob up on YouTube and find an old channel with just three videos. One of them is a presentation on alchemy spanning an hour and a half. I watch it carefully, left with mixed feelings. On the one hand, the information is brilliant. He's a good presenter and skillfully distills complex topics into simple, more accessible understandings. On the other hand, something about his mannerisms gives me pause: He seems over-postured and serious, a stark contrast to the easygoing, friendly guy I met earlier. I make a mental note and send him a text:

Just watched some of your alchemy content. Awesome stuff. Let's get together for a hike sometime.

Sounds good, he responds.

✦ ✦ ✦

Over the next few months, Rob and I exchange messages, trying to make plans, but nothing materializes. Then, in a strange turn of events, Rob moves to New Mexico and needs a place to camp. After a brief face-to-face meeting, I offer him a secluded spot on our property with a stunning view of the valley and mountains.

The late spring winds are still blowing strongly when Rob sets up camp with his furry companion. He improvises well, sleeping in his truck at first and then purchasing with the help of his mother a sturdy teepee-style canvas tent. He forms a good set-up on a sandy patch and builds a primitive kitchen around a stone-lined fire pit.

I know I'll be learning more than just alchemy from him. I'm curious about his personal evolution, especially since he's stopped practicing alchemy and adopted a more traditional biblical perspective. I also want to understand what happened with his business and what shifted his perspective.

A quick glance at his Instagram shows he ripped off a lot of people by collecting orders but not fulfilling them. Rumors on Reddit forums mention his strange behavior, declining product quality, and eventual disappearance. No one knew where he went. I seem to be one of the first to encounter him since he disappeared. So I know this will be a learning experience, even if it's not the ideal foundation for building a practice of alchemy.

I begin having regular "fire talks" with Rob. After work, I often go down to his tent to sit with him around the campfire. I learn that he's also a Leo, embodying the sun archetype. Despite this, Rob doesn't lean much into astrology. Instead, he seems intent on talking about how alchemy led him to what he considers the ultimate source of knowledge: the Bible. I listen patiently, absorbing what I can, but also gently try to steer the conversation back to alchemy when possible.

Over time, Rob opens up about his past. He tells me his mother abandoned him at a young age, leaving him to fend for himself in a nearby park. The story is hard to fully grasp, yet there's a pain in his eyes that makes me hesitate before dismissing it. I listen, trying to understand the roots.

Later, he recalls an experience at a college party where a

group of people were debating about what they thought was the truth about reality. "I said something like, 'I don't really know, but I think it's written in the Bible,' and everyone laughed at me," he says, expression dead serious.

He continues, "After that, I questioned everything. I was determined to find the truth, so I would have the answer. I studied all the world's religions until I eventually found alchemy. What drew me to it was that all its claims are testable. According to alchemy, all matter consists of three principle substances: oil, liquor, and salt. I researched everything I could get my hands on, and eventually, I tested it myself. And, indeed, I found the three principles to be true. That's how I knew I had found the truth."

Rob's story solidifies my confidence in alchemy, but it also raises a deep suspicion. Alchemy, while intellectually powerful, became a crutch rather than a tool to deeply connect with nature. This is a theme I've witnessed time and time again, across many disciplines: guru-type figures discovering a rich vein of thought and using it as an attempt to regain power they lost in their youth.

I share my thoughts with Meghan, and she says succinctly, "It sounds like he's searching for love."

My curiosity gets the best of me, so during our next fire talk, I ask him directly, "So, if alchemy proved to you to be the truth, why did you abandon it?"

"I walked that road to its end," he says. "I learned everything there was to know, accomplished all its goals, and had a multimillion-dollar business, but it corrupted me. Despite all the knowledge and success, I still felt empty and depressed. One day, I was high on psychedelics, sitting under a tree, and I saw a rainbow. I felt an overwhelming sense of clarity, and in that moment, I knew it was Jesus. He asked me if I would be his bride, and without hesitation, I agreed. I heard wedding bells, and in that instant, I understood that my alchemy career was over. It was as though a new chapter of my life had begun, one where I was saved by God."

"So what happened to your business?" I ask.

"I think my landlords were aliens," he says, matter-of-factly. "They tried multiple times to poison me and even hacked into my computer. Eventually, they called the cops, fabricated lies, and had me evicted from my unit. They even seized my truck and took my dog."

"How did you get your truck and dog back?" I ask, intrigued.

"I was camping in the woods when I ran into the sheriff. I had cured his family member of an illness, so he agreed to drop me off where my truck was impounded. I got there, and the guy demanded money to release my truck and dog. I didn't have any money, but then I felt a strange sensation in my pocket. I pulled out my wallet, and lo and behold, I had exactly the amount I needed to get them back."

"That's quite a story, man," I say, shaking my head in disbelief.

"Yeah," he responds, pausing for a beat. "God rescued me, but he took away my nature credit card," he laughs. "I'd racked up a lot of debt. As it turns out, I needed not only to be saved but totally re-educated. For the next year or so, I camped in different spots while God provided for me and taught me the truth. Now, I'm here, learning Hebrew in my free time, hanging with you."

I shoot the question: "Why do you think you are here?"

He straightens up, taking on a more rigid posture. "Probably to show you what happens when you walk this path to its end. It's dark. Only through Jesus can you enter the kingdom of God."

"Is it possible that I'm here to deliver you a message of some kind, too?" I ask, not trying to deflect but to soften the tone, and to remind myself not to devalue my own experience and power.

"I don't think so," he responds, his voice growing more firm. "My work now is about helping people see the truth in the Bible. There is no other word of God. That is the absolute truth, every word of it."

"I gotta be honest with you, Rob," I say. "I don't fully buy that. I have no doubt there's an incredible wealth of truth in the Bible, and I'm open to learning. But saying it's the absolute word of God assumes man channeled it purely. And not only that, countless generations of people have interpreted that message purely, free of any corruption."

"You're right. It has been corrupted. But the Jewish faith has done an exceptional job preserving the word of God. I trust in it."

"Okay, that may be so. I obviously have no idea. But there's another thing that prevents me from believing the Bible is the only word of God. From my experience, the word of God is also written in nature. It's all around us, within us, and we can access it if we choose to be receptive."

Rob visibly softens, both in posture and tone. "I agree with you on that," he says quietly. "I just think that the word of the Bible and the teachings of men make learning much more efficient."

I nod in agreement. "I can see where you are coming from. My experience is that nature is a masterful teacher. It's much slower, yes, but that slowness allows one to deeply process, step by step, and learn from the intelligence of God. But I know learning from nature isn't for everyone."

He gives a slight nod, and having found common ground, we shift into lighter conversation. We start speaking in alchemy metaphors of gold and mercury, a poetic language established by the alchemists of yore. The evening ends on a high note, in silence, as we sit across from one another. The fire blazes in between, casting beautiful golden light into the starry sky.

✦ ✦ ✦

Weeks pass, and the riddle that is Rob becomes even more complex. In the evenings, he's in his teepee, fully immersed in the Bible. During the day, he's crafting Native American bags adorned with the visionary geometric patterns that connect their culture to the Great Spirit.

Meghan observes that he seems like two different people, almost embodying an inner war between Christianity and Paganism, masculine and feminine. In his mind, he's clearly chosen the former. But in his actions—weaving bags and speaking fondly of nature—he embodies the latter. And, frankly, he's a lot more pleasant to be around and seems more authentic when he's in this more feminine state.

As I struggle to reconcile these opposites within him, I try to understand his perspective on the Bible. I read passages and stories, especially drawn to the one about the prophet who shares my name, Daniel. I find it fascinating how Daniel has visions, how his truth is tested when the king throws him into a pit of lions.

I keep an open mind, finding much in the biblical stories that resonates with me. Meghan, on the other hand, is skeptical. Not so much of the Bible but of Rob himself. She shares with me her sense that he looks down on women, that he's made her feel belittled on multiple occasions. She's confused by the extremes of his dual nature and suspicious of the truthfulness of his stories. She feels that he's trying to dominate me, that he's competing with her for my attention.

I take heed of Meghan's concerns. While I still value the insights I extract from Rob's alchemical experience, I grow weary of his constant warnings about alchemy, as if he knows my fate with certainty. He obviously has an agenda to convert me to his way of thinking. No direct conflicts, as I simply stand firm in my core understandings, not engaging in much debate with him, but there's a quiet disconnect growing between us.

When Meghan and I return from our honeymoon, Rob tells us that his mom is moving to New Mexico, and he's going to be moving in with her, taking a job as a landscaper. I can tell he's really determined to step into a more masculine role as well as repair his relationship with his mother. We all agree that it's for the best that he moves on.

✦ ✦ ✦

During the following months, I reflect on the role that Rob played in my learning process. I've learned that alchemy is the language of the stars, and if this star-level knowledge is not grounded in a mission to serve all of nature, it becomes a path of self-inflation. A means to assert superiority over others. This can make us feel like we are above nature, positioning our small mind as omniscient instead of a bridge between nature and the space of dreams. And this so often leads to emptiness and eventual self-destruction.

This pattern of disembodiment, of loss of connection to nature leading to destruction, is something I've seen not just in personalities, but also in countless stories. In fairy tales as well as modern myths. In culture, from Wall Street to Hollywood. And now, even in Rob, who still holds a connection to nature, but doesn't truly believe in it. Perhaps the fast track he was on, ushered in by books instead of a communication with nature, was too much for him to handle. The fast track is not always the right one.

I came to see Rob as both a cautionary tale and a teacher whose path had crossed mine for a reason. He offered me a glimpse of what can happen when the language of the stars is pursued without the grounding wisdom of the Earth. I certainly learned more about the Bible than I had before meeting him, and we shared many fruitful conversations about alchemy and nature. My younger self might have been more receptive to Rob's authoritative stance and narrative, but experience kept me anchored in a story that felt deeper and more meaningful to me: the dream of nature. With that anchor, I was able to remain centered and confident in my own path. For that, I feel proud of myself.

Yet still, Rob's absence leaves a void in my learning process about alchemy. Though I consider nature my primary teacher, there is truth in what Rob said: Other people can help make the learning process more efficient. I seek a balance of both learning sources, and so I find myself searching for another alchemy teacher. I had been engaging in light discussion with two established alchemy practitioners online, but I find myself at a crossroads on whom to pursue. I decide to let nature guide the way.

I'm back in the Rocky Mountains, not far from the spot where I learned the lesson in gratitude from the river. This time, I'm high up on a cliff overlooking the valley. It's a gorgeous early summer day, and the mountainsides are painted in swathes of vivid green leaves. I've already spent most of the day roaming the peaks. Now I'm sitting in a peaceful spot, half-meditating, half-soaking in the beauty around me.

I close my eyes, expecting blackness or the light fractal patterns I see sometimes in a deeply relaxed state. Instead, I see a mosaic of color, like I'm looking into a moving stained-glass lamp. I recognize the contours of the fleur de lis pattern, flapping like a butterfly. But now it's sharper, more defined. As I focus, I see it clearly: an angel, spreading its wings, made of pure geometric light rays.

As I sit in awe and stillness, I ask the angel its name.

"Gabriella," it replies.

A part of me wonders if I've heard that name before, maybe from Gabriel, the male angel in the Bible. But Gabriella speaks again:

"Angels don't have a gender. We come in the form that best suits the people we help."

I think back to Vermont when I would close my eyes and see the vague shapes of winged animals flying. To see now, with crystalline clarity, that it was an angel is a profound awakening.

I decide to put this revelation to the test. I tell Gabriella the names of two teachers I'm considering, Sky and Raven, and ask her which one I should choose.

Her form fades, and I open my eyes. Almost immediately, I see a black bird, probably a crow, across the valley. It's flying away from me, though, and stirs a sense of unease. I hear Gabriella's voice again in my mind.

"Look up."

I lean back against the rocks behind me, shifting my gaze up to the perfectly blue sky, laced with puffy clouds. A nostalgic feeling washes over me, reminding me of the innocence I had when I was a child. And at that moment, I know that Sky is the one who will guide me through the laboratory practice of alchemy.

With that knowledge, I have another revelation: Rob had unlocked something within, allowing me to connect with an angel for the first time. I let the weight of that settle. Then, I thank Rob for opening that doorway for me.

And with that revelation, I now understand that my teachers exist both above and below, within the stars and the soil, in the abstract world of imagination and the living terrain of nature, including the human realm. I see them all as different forms, different voices, but all arising from the same living field of creation.

They are each like threads within the vast mind of The Dreamer—a surreal terrain where finite lifetimes unfold inside the infinite dream we call nature. By opening myself to the collective intelligence of this vast mind, my own mind becomes an instrument of nature instead of an echo chamber.

From this more etheric perspective, I no longer fixate on the form truth takes when it arrives. What matters is that I keep tracking it, allowing nature's alchemical pressure and elemental intelligence to shape my way forward and transform me as I go. Each vision, inner revelation, and inspired action becomes another marker on the trail, and another small piece of treasure gathered along the way.

For now, that's enough to keep me tracking.

And if you're following nature's call too, I'll see you on the trail.

If you'd like to join me, plus explore the tools that emerged along the way you can find them here:

www.spiritualperformance.net

If the book resonated with you, one of the most helpful things you can do is leave a short review.

www.spiritualperformance.net/review